HOW CAN I REWIRE MY BRAIN WITH POSITIVE THINKING

Ilary J. Powell

Contents

Chapter One

INTRODUCTION

Anxiety disorder is a generalized term that is intended to cover a wide range of fears and tensions. Therapists as of now have a wide scope of various analytic methodology to decide the nearness of anxiety disorders. Studies have discovered that as much as 18% of the populace in America experiences at least one of these anxiety disorders.

Anxiety disorders are frequently a chronic issue for sufferers. They can exhibit at an early age or can all of a sudden show up after a horrible mishap that triggers them. Anxiety assault regularly erupt during critical increments in stress and are frequently joined by physical indications, for example, migraines, muscle fits, perspiring, hypertension, and heart palpitations. In serious cases, individuals that experience the ill effects of significant anxiety and panic disorders have extreme issues with weakness and now and again depletion.

In like manner discourses, anxiety and dread are frequently utilized conversely. Nonetheless, in clinical talks, they are altogether different and have their own unmistakable definitions. Anxiety is known as an emotional state that is extremely unsavory and has no conclusive reason. Regularly anxiety is believed to be wild and there is no real way to keep away from the side effects. Dread, then again, is an emotional and mental reaction to a danger that exists inside the earth. Anxiety disorder is a blend of tensions and fears together. Fears are a noteworthy shared trait in anxiety disorders.

Anxiety attacks are normally alluded to as anxiety attacks. Individuals that experience the ill effects of these disorders have numerous noteworthy medical issues and difficulties. Panic attacks have an exceptionally abrupt beginning. They make exceptional anxiety sentiments. There are regularly no immediate triggers of such infection. They please abruptly and all of a sudden. Panic attacks incorporate indications that incorporate serious dread, steamed stomach, and other physical distresses. There are likewise indications and practices related with panic attacks that influence an individual's capacity to work typically in the public arena.

The side effects identified with such illness regularly keep going for around thirty minutes. Be that as it may, a few attacks keep going for a couple of moments. A few occurrences of panic attacks are the aftereffect of a continuous situation so the panic attacks will happen for expanded timeframes. Frequently, individuals that are experiencing panic attacks will have exceptional times of anxiety where they envision the attacks and will have negligible help between their out and out panic attacks. Numerous individuals that experience the ill effects of anxiety attacks find that they have a sentiment of being caught and not having the option to liberate themselves from a terrible circumstance.

Chapter Two

How does brain work

The mind works just like a significant computerkeyboard. It processes information it receives from the body and senses, and also sends messages back into your system. However, the brain could do considerably more than the usual system may: humans feel and feel emotions using their own brain, and it's the origin of individual intellect.

The human mind is about the magnitude of 2 clenched fists and weighs around 1.5 kilograms. From the surface it looks a little like a massive walnut, together with cracks and folds. Brain cells is composed of roughly 100 billion nerve cells (neurons) plus something billion encouraging cells that stabilize the tissues.

There are various parts of their mind, each using their particular purposes:

· the cerebrum

· the diencephalon -- like the thalamus, hypothalamus and adrenal gland

· the brain stem cells -- like the midbrain, pons and medulla

· the cerebellum

Structure of the mind

The cerebrum includes a ideal half and a left half, called the left and right hemispheres. Both hemispheres are attached using a thick bundle of nerve fibers called the corpus callosum.

Each hemisphere is composed of six areas (lobes) which have various purposes. The cerebrum controls movement and processes sensory data. Conscious and subconscious feelings and actions are all produced here. It's also in charge of language, hearing, memory and intellect.

The purposes of both hemispheres will be to a fantastic degree different: whereas the left hemisphere is in charge of language and abstract thinking from a lot of people, the ideal structure is normally accountable for spatial believing or vision. The ideal side of this brain controls the left side of their body, and also the remaining side of this brain controls the ideal side of their human body. Which usually means that injury to the left hemisphere because of stroke, as an instance, may cause paralysis to the ideal side of their human anatomy.

The remaining cerebral cortex is in charge of language and speech. The ideal cerebral cortex provides spatial facts, like where your foot are at this time. The thalamus stipulates that the cerebrum with sensory information by the eyes, ears and eyes, in addition to additional info. The hypothalamus modulates things such as thirst, hunger and sleep. Along with the adrenal gland, in addition, it modulates the hormones in the system.

The mind stem cells information between your mind, the cerebellum and the back, in addition to controlling eye movements and facial expressions. Additionally, it regulates vital functions like breathing, blood pressure and pulse.

The cerebellum coordinates moves and accounts for balance.

The remaining cerebral cortex is responsible for language and speech. The ideal cerebral cortex provides spatial facts, like where your foot are at this time. The thalamus stipulates that the cerebrum with sensory information by the eyes, ears and eyes, in addition to additional info. The hypothalamus modulates things such as thirst, hunger and sleep. Along with the adrenal gland, in addition, it modulates the hormones in the system.

The mind stem cells information between your mind, the cerebellum and the back, in addition to controlling eye movements and facial expressions. Additionally, it regulates vital functions like breathing, blood pressure and pulse.

The cerebellum coordinates moves and accounts for balance.

What's the brain provided with blood?

The mind needs a steady stream of sufficient oxygen, sugar, along with other nourishment. Because of this, it's a especially excellent blood source. All sides of the mind receives blood flow through three cells:

· at front, the lateral cerebral artery provides the tissue supporting the forehead and under the summit (at the top of the mind).

· the middle cerebral artery is also very important to both areas and sides which can be further in your brain. The anterior and middle cerebral artery divide removed by the internal carotid artery, a significant arteries in the throat.

· the anterior cerebral artery provides the rear of the mind, the reduced portion of their brain, and also the cerebellum. It's supplied with blood vessels in the thoracic arteries, which can be also major blood vessels of the throat.

Before the 3 cells hit"their" mind area, where they divide into smaller branchesthey have been close together below the brain. Inside this region, they're linked to one another by smaller blood-stream forming a structure much like a traffic group. The arteries are attached to eachother in different areas too. The benefit of these links is the blood distribution trouble in mental perfor-mance can be paid for to a certain degree: as an instance, in case a division of the artery gradually becomes thinner, blood may flow into the com-ponent of the brain that it provides through those other avenues (collateral blood flow).

The tiniest branches (capillaries) of the blood vessels from the mind provide the mind cells with nourishment and oxygen from the bloodstream -- however they usually do not enable different chemicals pass as readily as similar cells in the remaining portion of your human body perform. The clinical term for this happening may be that the"blood-brain barrier" it helps protect the fragile mind from toxic chemicals in the bloodstream, such as.

After oxygen has passed in to the cells, then the more oxygen-poor blood flows out throughout the veins of their brain (cerebral tissue). The veins carry blood flow into larger bloodstream called sinuses. The nasal walls have been reinforced by way of a tough membrane (dura mater), which helps them maintain their shape too. This keeps them eternally open and causes it to be simple for that blood flow to the veins at the throat.

Every creature you can consider -- mammals, reptiles, fish, reptiles, amphibians -- features a brain. Nevertheless, the mind is exceptional.

Even though it is perhaps not the biggest, it gives us the capability to speak, imagine and problem solve. It's really an remarkable organ.

The mind plays with an amazing number of jobs involving these:

The mind controls your skill to think, speak, feel, and watch, listen, remember things, walk plus far more. It controls your breathing.

The mind is a muscle mass of supportive nerves and tissues linked into the back. A number of those nerves inside the mind move directly into the eyes, eyes and other regions of the pinnacle. Different nerves connect the brain along with different pieces of the human body via the back to restrain disposition, body and senses works by breathing .

In addition, the brain, spinal cord and nerves form the central nervous system.

Researching how the mind and spinal cord work helps you understand brain tumors:

Exactly what a brain cyst consists of

The observable signs of brain tumors

The way the brain cyst can be diagnosed

The way the brain cyst can be medicated

Brain-stem

The cerebrum

Even the cerebrum, the big, outer part of the mind, controls studying, believing, learning, language, emotions and intended muscle moves like walking. Additionally, it controls vision, hearing and other senses.

The cerebrum is divided two cerebral hemispheres (halves): right and left. The ideal half controls the remaining part of their human body. The remaining half controls the ideal side of their human body.

Each structure contains four sections, called lobes: frontal, parietal, rectal along with occipital. Each lobe controls special purposes. By way of instance, the frontal lobe controls nature, reasoning and decision-making, whilst the temporal lobe controls, memory, language, and sense of smell.

The cerebellum

Even the cerebellum, at the back of the mind, controls equilibrium, co ordination and muscle control (e.g., walking). Additionally, it works to maintain equilibrium and posture.

The mind stem

The brain-stem , at the base of the mind, joins the cerebrum with the spinal-cord . It features that the mid brain , the pons, and also the medulla. It controls fundamental human body functions like breathing, and eye movementsand blood pressure, heartbeat, as well as consuming.

Fixing the central nervous system

Due to the fragility of their brain and spinal cord, the body has a built-in defense mechanisms against injury.

The skull as well as the meninges -- that the liner of the mind -- protect the mind, whereas the bones of the spine protect the spinal cord, and the fluid surrounds and cushions the brain and the back.

The skull is the bony frame of this mind comprised of 2-1 bones. The cranium, the component of the skull which insures the brain, is composed of four big bones: frontal, occipital, rectal and also parietal. The skull the nasal shelf, is created from a intricate collection of bones which also interact with all the bones of their throat and face. There are other bones at the cranium: 2 rectal bones, about both sides and bottom of their skull, and 2 connective bones, on very top of the skull.

Even the meninges are 3 layers of tissue. The surface coating, the dura mater, is thick and thick just like leather. The third and second coats, that the arachnoid and also pia mater, are lean.

Cerebrospinal fluid is a liquid fluid which flows in and round the four different portions of the brain (called ventricles) and the spinal cord, also between 2 of the meninges. The ventricles are attached.

The way the brain works: the pieces of the brain

Our mind is a set of different parts that have to learn how to come together. To help explain this, neuro-physiologist," dr. Paul maclean, who led the national government lab of brain development, is rolling out the idea of an evolution-ary"triune" brain arrangement into his revolutionary book,"the triune brain in evolution."

At the peak of the backbone we've got a brain stem. Atone point in development of vertebrates that is the brain the organism needed. It's frequently known as the reptilian brain. The majority of our automatic and instinctual responses (flee or fight, etc.) Originate from the mind.

Additionally entirely on the rear side of their brainstem may be that the cerebellum, a early portion of the brain in an evolutionary perspective, which is accountable to its sub-conscious grasp of most muscle moves.

In addition to the brainstem, profound within the cerebral cortex, can be available next thing in development, the crude mammalian brain, frequently recognized because the limbic lobes. The brain is available in most mammals including probably the many primitive mammal. This is actually the chair of the emotional reactions.

As mammals became highly evolved, they also developed an cerebral cortex enclosing the brain. This is really where our logical thinking is all also, voluntary muscle building, centres for vision and other sensations.

When you look in a frontal perspective of mental performance, it resembles a huge walnut. The mind has a profound notch running from front to rear. It resembles half an shelled walnut. So from the cerebral stage we all now have exactly what are called right and left brain hemispheres.

The nerves operating involving the entire body and mental performance crossover from the medulla (an integral part of the brain stem cells) therefore that the left hemisphere is connected with the ideal side of their physique and the ideal hemisphere with the remaining portion side. Between both hemispheres we've a narrow communicating bridge which we predict a corpus callosum.

We will need to communicate between those two pliers for several pursuits. The left quadrant we are able to predict the linear logic speech

. The ideal hemisphere is the visual and visual incorporating quadrant. The left hemisphere is reductionist and finds that our universe as little pieces and bits, and also the ideal hemisphere sees the big picture. Western civilization is mostly left-brained, and also oriental civilization is primarily right handed.

The mind is a very intricate and sometimes mysterious organ of the body. There are not many people who know exactly the way this penis actually works. A whole lot of people frequently wonder how it's that a few individuals have massive iq degrees and a few others struggle with all the simplest activities.

I guess one excuse that's been passed is the brain is the same as a muscle from your system. The further you work the muscle that the longer it develops. So the further you utilize your brain then your longer it's going to get the job done with youpersonally. Which usually means that should you not use the human brain alot afterward it will fight to deal with plenty of things.

The connection with all the muscular endings there however. Because unlike the muscle which gets poorer as we get old, the brain may function quite well but continue to have the ability to ingest information together with era. In addition, due to that the further you study afterward a higher your brain will work.

Reading may also be an excellent instrument for arousing the mind. That is only because you are reading you in many cases are placing the human brain in to unchartered waters because you will never know what's coming up .

Finding the mind to completely know what's happening from the novel and connecting it to the exterior world is just another intricate way in that the individual brain works. It needs to decode symbols and words that we know just what's happening.

Therefore if you're looking to increase your own iq you ought to occupy reading. The further that you give the human brain to complete the longer it's going to get the job done with youpersonally. Don't allow the human brain stay idle because it can be no good because of this whatsoever. The further work that you simply make the human mind do the higher it's going to have the ability to find the details you seek.

Knowing the way the mind functions and exactly what makes it tick is really a intricate subject. People experienced their thoughts regarding any of it and there are a few weird and terrific insights to the way a mind works. The mind is quite a mysterious manhood really.

Many have inquired how many folks can attain high iq degrees and a few may not even be able to make a move quite straightforward and possess very low iq degrees.

Well some folks have likened the brain into muscles. It is said that the further you utilize your own brain and induce it to get the job done afterward your longer it'll grow. The people with all the low iq levels are not likely setting their brain to act as they need to do. Exactly enjoy the muscular, in case you work hard in muscle tissue they'll necessarily grow stronger.

Therefore essentially the longer amount of period you just spend analyzing the further the human mind will ultimately grow and also the brainier you may get. An odd issue is that if the muscles will fundamentally weaken because you become old, the mind may still maintain its capacity to know once we grow older.

Reading is a really good way to excite your mind. That is only because you are reading the human brain is constantly working all of the time to work out exactly what's happening.

The mind must make the relationship between exactly what it really is reading and what's in the actual life and decode the symbols and messages so. A area of the brain is working all of the opportunity in order to produce you grasp what's happening as you're reading.

Therefore it's natural to presume that should you want to increase your iq level hen it's a fantastic concept to begin reading more. Always work to provide the mind some thing to perform and make sure it remains active.

Before you improve your memory the very first step is always to find out how it worksout. For memory there's an activity that your brain undergoes at which it acquires or arranges in coming info, consolidates and forms which advice and in a subsequent time you possess that capability to remember the information that's been stored and acquired.

This really is really a procedure for the mind and the nervous system working together, also it comprises two forms of information: comprehension and procedures.

Certainly one of the simplest methods to enhance your memory is regularly using it! You certainly can achieve so is by attempting to think otherwise or remember what you never have considered in quite a while. Employing little games such as remembering every creature you can think of beginning with a specific letter, or even virtually every country you've seen (useful in case you're well travelled!) . That is known as bending your memory and in fact it leaves it increasingly nimble. Exactly like a muscle, the more you exercise it that the larger it's!

Another thing that's been demonstrated to improve your memory is always learning a new language. This exercises your own mind by exposing it into new, unknown words and sounds your brain is going to be made to absorb and retain. The absolute level of information demanded in learning a new language will undoubtedly help the human brain exercises and better your m emory... Maybe not forgetting the way that it'll enhance your communication abilities.

New research also indicate that carrying short naps throughout your daytime enriches memory.

At the start of sleep an interval of communicating begins which fosters your memory.

Together with 80-100 billion nerve cells, called neurons, the individual mind is with the capacity of any astonishing feats. Each neuron is linked to greater than 1000 other neurons, which makes the entire quantity of links in the mind around 60 trillion! Neurons are arranged into networks and patterns within the mind and keep in touch with one another at incredible rates.

How do experiments get the job done?

Each neuron is composed of three chief components: the body (also called the soma), the axon, and also the dendrites. Neurons communicate together using electro chemical signs. To put it differently, certain compounds in the human body called ions have a electric charge. Ions move around in and outside of this neuron on the other side of the cell membrane and also change the electric control of the neuron.

If a neuron is at rest, the body, or soma, of this neuron is negatively charged in accordance with the beyond this neuron. A neuron in the rest has a poor control of approximately -70 millivolts (mv) of power. But as soon as a stimulation comes together (such as stubbing your toe, or hearing the name being called)it causes the neuron to simply take in more favorable ions, and also the neuron will become positively charged. Once the neuron reaches a particular threshold of approximately -55mv, a conference called an action potential occurs and leads to the neuron to"fire" the action potential travels down the axon at which it reaches the axon terminal.

At the axon terminal, the electric signals are changed to chemical signs that traveling between nerves along a tiny gap called the synapse. These compounds are called neurotransmitters. Neuro-transmitters cross the synapse and attach to receptors in the dendrites of neurons that are nearby. Dendrites are all branch-like projections which take impulses received from nearby volunteers into the soma

What's mental performance organized?

Neurotransmitters are not the same as ions, because rather than straight affecting the charge of these nerves, neurotransmitters communicate with triggering a receptor. To put it differently, the neurotransmitter is similar to a secret and also the receptor could be your lock. Once the"main" turns out the"lock," or once the neurotransmitter attaches to the receptor, then the material is passed and also the receptors are recycled. The transmission of information from neuron to neuron, also between networks of volunteers, gives rise to all from believing to playing sport, solving issues, and maybe dreaming.

Neurons from the brain and spinal cord are all coordinated in to the peripheral and central nervous systems. Even the central nervous system is coordinated into different operational areas:

1)) the neo cortex, that can be coordinated to lobes found from the case below.

Two) the neostriatum or basal ganglia, that may be seen deep within the arrangement.

3) the diencephalon, that comprises both the thalamus and hypothalamusand can be additionally found deep within your mind.

4) the brain stem.

5) the back cable.

Often times, distinct lobes and areas come together to perform complicated behaviours such as learning or talking. Not only are those neurons always communicating with one another, however in addition they interact with volunteers from the peripheral nervous system.

The peripheral nervous system consists of motor and sensory nerves across the remainder of one's entire body. The sensory nerves collect information from the outside world during the five senses, whereas the engine neurons enable one to maneuver and respond to signals in the brain and back.

Once you're born, then you'd nearly all the nerves you'll ever have, and also a lot more sensory connections compared to you personally have now. The mind continues to grow and change during the life as the relations between nerves are all plastic. To put it differently, your mind may incorporate new relations or subtract ones that are unused. Since you develop, your experiences and surroundings help the human mind pick which links are useful and important. Besides your own experiences, genetic advice too influences the human mind's evolution. Even though it is extremely complex to tease apart what's inherited and what's heard, many behaviours seem to become considered a combination of both environmental and genetic elements.

Chapter Three

Change mental paradigm

Each one of us comes with a specific perspective of earth. Though our perspective could possibly be like the others, and there could be matters a massive set comes in common, each and each of us has our own special view and perspective of matters of the way they truly are and how they work.

We're all victims of particular thought patterns, and such routines or paradigm dictate substantially our perspective of earth and also the way we work on earth. We have to keep an eye on these paradigm and work toward breaking them out and allowing us to start and receive new thoughts and perspectives.

These paradigm have consistently existed through out most human presence, and also have for ages been shown to be wrong, or maybe not entirely accurate. The planet is level, god is mad every time a solar panel comes to pass, the sun goes across the ground.

These are paradigm of societies during history which have been ordinary beliefs, but recognized to be incorrect. We all hold our very own paradigm about the world and also how things work. We utilize those paradigm to work from the planet and exist on an everyday basis, but we must comprehend why these paradigm's frequently times limit us are perhaps not the entire picture.

Paradigm's are really not just a terrible thing. Our thoughts and beliefs on the planet are the things let us navigate the entire world along with work. We've got paradigm regarding our responsibilities as spouses, parents, worker etc. These paradigm help us comprehend the way we are to work on the planet.

What we have to be careful of though is becoming trapped in such paradigm limiting ourselves within our power to enlarge and reach more. When western society thought that the universe was flat and also an explorer could fall off the edge of the planet, western society limited itself into investigating and detecting lands which weren't yet part of their own reality. This is before christophercolumbus chose never to trust the paradigm and also utterly shattered western societies notion relating to it.

We must learn how to explore outdoors our very personal paradigm beliefs also. This really could be the only real way we'll ever start to enlarge about that which we are able to consume, do, and also become inside our lives. Our paradigm are our perspectives of earth, plus so they let us navigate, thus we have to learn how to enlarge the map as we'd purchase a fresh roadmap when an older one was outside obsolete.

A lot of people out there assert that the law of attraction is either satanic or perhaps a lot of bull and can not get the job done. This might or might not be accurate, but i do not agree because i've seen it work again and again. The purpose is that a number folks are not able to tag something without requiring the opportunity to comprehend it and return to your own decisions, only as a result our private paradigm.

We could see this in kids as a perfect instance. Many kids might find some thing their parents do not prefer to eat in reunite pick they don't really enjoy it . Or they'll just won't eat something as they're of the opinion they don't really enjoy it. Even if they've not eaten itthey have been convinced that they don't really enjoy it.

I visit it within my children every one of the moment and in grownup as well. People today become stuck into a paradigm about some thing and eventually become convinced that their design would be your reality. We have to be careful and aware and let ourselves research so as to figure out whether the paradigm we grip demands advancing, or whether our present paradigm concerning it's true enough to benefit all of us.

Most of all, we must constantly, always understand our existing paradigm is not complete rather than 100% true. Nothing we believe would be the entire film, and not one of our present paradigm are completely true concerning whatever else. Work toward enlarging your own paradigm and start up yourself to get new thoughts and new paradigm, then being a grownup, pick whether the paradigm shift may function you personally or never.

What is a paradigm? It's a pair of mental perspectives and beliefs in a place of one's own life. Your emotional paradigm will specify things such as just how much it is possible to perform in this area, just how much enjoyment you choose as a result, of course in the event that you carry on to evolve into your comprehension of it or never. This guide is going to reveal to you everything it really means to alter your paradigm, and also the worlds it might available for your requirements.

A paradigm change is an essential measure on your spiritual growth, and a paradigm shift definition will probably be essential for you as it is going to provide you a sense about what you're going through in regards to maneuver. I gives an even more daily example, after which we can chat about the way this pertains to spirituality.

Let us say you've got to perform a project that you despise. That you never find a way to avoid it, and also your only solution would be always to continue arriving daily. 1 day you get up and understand you never need to accomplish it . There is a point in which you view chances and manners out there are under your nose the entire time, you just beg to them. Nothing changed on your circumstances in 1 morning into another location, what changed was you personally. This is actually a paradigm shift definition.

Just how does this affect spirituality?

The exact same procedure also applies to our religious lifestyles. Our own internal growth travel might be long and difficult. We've to juggle inner work together with tasks, children, marriage, and also the countless of different activities that help keep us busy. We can get rid of steam to get our spiritual pursuit, and we all know it we forget the reason we started outside within the first location. Just how is really a predicament in this way in regard to your inner work just like a terrible job situation?

The solution is it is the very same. A paradigm you made yourself likely has blocked you out of internal expansion, from fresh methods of handling brand new responsibilities. Some times it can look as if that our spiritual growth is placed on hold to manage the pressures of lifeand also this really is every time a paradigm shift definition tends to kick some openings at the walls of the prisons and create new doors to all of us. This shift could possibly be a fresh spiritual understanding that incorporates our daily life together with your spiritual growth, or even perhaps a brand new fire within our hearts which makes us wake up one hour earlier each day to provide the time and energy to our own selves.

Require action

Have a minute today and believe about almost any aspects of your life where your spirit is hungry for further attention. Simply take this fresh paradigm shift definition and examine the ways that your emotional attitudes or paradigms are preventing you by opening new doors of opportunity on your spiritual development. Things to keep an eye out to get a lightness of soul, or even a sense of freedom, in addition to the responses you were searching for. Trust these despite the fact that they might appear improbable, as you're going to take the middle of a paradigm shift.

Here's really a celestial dialogue to expand your thoughts about loyalty, truth, change and that you're comparative to divinity. A invitation to step in to creatorship. Key ideas are italicised.

We come ahead we encounter ahead here voluntarily, happily, exuberantly. Perhaps not to guide youpersonally, nor to direct youpersonally, nor to demonstrate how. We're extremely aware - because we all participate with the collective field - of that which we now could call a fresh paradigm appearing. Consistently paradigms own application, or utilize, or significance on quite a few distinct areas of one's own lives. A paradigm is more deeper compared to the usual position in different words. A paradigm can be deeper than an situation. A paradigm is the way you translate your situation, and also make sense of your own issues. And therefore that while we recognise and honor which the actions, the churning, the problems, the events which exist in the context of one's own lives are all important, and worth discussing, expressinglearning , we have to say that without altering on the degree of paradigm, regardless of true change ever does occur from the situation . They could seem different a couple of months or even perhaps a couple of years on, however the basis of the struggle, or even the strain, or even perhaps the block, or even the escape, whatever it can be, will probably soon be precisely the same.

Therefore because we come ahead - not signifi-cantly, maybe not using sombreness, or severity, and sometimes not with fantastic reverence - we all come forward here , thankfully, exuberantly and we all desire to start for you a paradigmatic hint. As always that is simply a proposal, only an invitation to that you're welcome to state no or yes and there'll not be a lack of passion for you personally from the universe. There'll not be a less endorsement, no proposed decision and punishment, based on whether you just take this invitation up. We know that may become your adventure of love, but that's perhaps not just how we love. So what we attract is only, and only an invitation.

It's to do with that which you believe you are, comparative to god. Today you may assume that aspect has nothing or little related to the problems and the situation where you're grappling within this phase on your own practical, regular lifestyles. We're speaking for you it's what related to this.

Frequent paradigms - the puppet

If we can, we'll discuss a few of the ordinary paradigms which can be observable in this civilization within this moment. Paradigms around who humans are comparative to god, ms.. There are several different belief systems, lots of diverse methods of earning sense of the. And humanity is growing in such. However, what exactly is visible in this phase, within this particular culture, and that'll consequently have impacted you , are such 2 models.

The very first is that the version of this historically, in which god or the universe (it cann't matter exactly the terminology, it's the paradigm that's crucial, not the pruning of items) is regarded as responsible. Not accountable from the older way of contemplating it for example sending lightning bolts as punishment. Perhaps today it's understood that god is currently accountable for by sending disorder because bad or punishment occurrences of some type. It's merely the exact same as believing in a god that directs lightning as punishment, even if you feel that disorder can be punitive somehow. That really is actually the paradigm, the concept that an increased force is responsible for all. What happens on earth may be that the will of this greater force and you also must only play with the match as best you can within the limits of one's own fate as designed with this higher force.

Those individuals from the paradigm, from the puppet mindset, could most likely say such things as:"it had been supposed to be more", or"it was not intended to be more", or"at god's time", aspects such as this. Perhaps not every time those phrases are clubbed are they from an puppet paradigm, maybe not in all, not in all. There's also truth round the facet of elegance, not forcing item on the planet, but being receptive to a pure rhythm and which will be a extremely empowered posture. But some times those phrases are suggesting that the individual uttering them is surviving in a paradigm.

The consequences of residing in this paradigm - and it should not be always, it might just be some times - so are quite obvious; a lower sense of responsibility, a lower sense of ability, an knowing that whatever you have needs to be got, your point in life has to be seen, you must think it is and search it, then obey it. Those sorts of thoughts result in puppet paradigm.

When we predict it puppet paradigm, we now are making it a caricature, an extreme method of saying what we mean within this paradigm. Although perhaps not many men and women that live out with the paradigm are of necessity unintelligent, perhaps not all of are unspiritual, a number of them may actually be somewhat spiritual, however you will notice by the working in these lifestyles, their capacity to create what they really want - and that's this is of power - can be relatively very low. The issue isn't their intellect, the issue isn't karma, the dilemma isn't spirituality, the issue could be the paradigm.

The secondly shared paradigm: the student

Ordinarily - because paradigms operate on an evolutionary foundation also - some time afterwards residing in nordic paradigm, a person being will start to flirt with the dynamics of this student at which rather than divinity being in control, in the place of divinity being a puppet master," it's currently the teacher and also a individual may be your student. That's the student paradigm.

Individuals that are indulged in this paradigm - and you can find quite many now - will most likely talk alot about the courses within their own lives . They'll believe they are on our earth to know, that the program is pre determined and their occupation is really always to work though courses 1 by 1 that they will soon be rewarded with continuing forward to the following semester. That's a really common mythology right now.

We'll never predict some of them paradigms erroneous. Noticewe have never stated that. They aren't erroneous, but they may be out-grown . At a particular point in your own life, becoming mindful of the puppet mentality might be rather helpful for you personally. It might bring you a bit of peace, it can provide you trust, it might let you to get through a circumstance, or even perhaps a youth, since it regularly does. There are occasions from the human travel when that paradigm is more right, however it only isn't adequate. You may grow your path outside of this being truly a helpful version in which to know your connection with god. And should you not allow your self - also it's really tough - however should you not let yourself alter your fundamental paradigm whenever you have out grown it, then there's no way it's possible to alter, essentially alter the conditions of one's daily life . Once we said earlier in the day, you are only going to circulate in just a paradigm you've actually outgrown, however, can't grab your self to leave behind.

Hence the pupil paradigm isn't erroneous, in reality it's a constructive development when some body allows themselves to maneuver out of their puppet paradigm, and then into the student . There's slightly more responsibility drawn from the student paradigm than that there was from the puppet. However, the essence of the duty is about learning. That's the phrase that's used, it's the mindset, and so it will become how what's observed.

In this specific paradigm individuals are often quite committed. They work quite difficult on themselves. They're reflective a-lot , perhaps some times a lot of. They get very observant of these, however maybe not therefore willing to accept risks. That's a portion of what this means to participate in this student paradigm. Also people utilize that paradigm to describe the reason why they don't really make real changes :"i need to learn about the lesson ", can be uttered inside this paradigm, so"i am not adjusting this, or creating different things, or leaving behind, because i simply have not heard it ".

Therefore, as with paradigms, it is not erroneous, however at a specific period of your journey it will become a limiting theory, rather than an enabling individual . Whenever you're only extending right into responsibility, and outside of victimhood, afterward it had been of use that you simply take up on you that the student paradigm. Nonetheless, it isn't the fullest truth. And we'd encourage you to test your self very closely with regard to the method that you employ both of these paradigms, in the situations you revert into them, and the way you could really be concealing them behind. This isn't a intellectual evaluation, but it's an easy truth-telling physical exercise.

But it's deeply frightening to some human being allowing their paradigm around god to alter changeor expand in any substantial manner . It seems blasphemous, it seems wrong, it seems irreverent. More than this, in the event that you create adaptation into a view about that which you're comparative to god, maybe making a mockery of how you've lived for the last couple of decades, and that will not feel great. But that is the reason why we assert for youpersonally, the paradigms - do not require - that they aren't erroneous. These certainly were of good use for you personally at that moment, they've become out grown.

Therefore you can return to some stage in your own life as soon as your relationship to god was different and also you may still recognise, respect, and honor that during that time it had been crucial and helpful that you participate with divinity so, if you had been doing this consciously, or unconsciously. And today you may possibly have discovered a brand new paradigm which has a far better influence you. Because that is what we want to get here: perhaps not reality but impact of a truth.

Judge some thing with its own effect, perhaps not by everything you deem to function as'truth'

There's no manner, while you're within a mind, you will know the complete truth with a capital . It's maybe not the look. In consenting expressing yourself , this can be a marvellous doubts, you agree to withhold or suspend, full comprehension. You're not likely to be aware of the entire film about divinity, or even lifetime, or even humankind if not your self as you're living and phys-ical in duality. But do you really should . It isn't too life is your constant search for truth with all the capital , it's for one to make use of, and also we state utilize, whatever reality functions best for you anytime of one's own life, whatever real-ity feels like you personally the very honouring, probably the very thrilling, and gets got the most useful effect you.

Judge a fact, or even a concept, or a idea, or perhaps a belief or true for this thing, by its own effect on you personally. When a notion puts you free, more happy than you before, whether it grants you slightly more energy, ex-citement, enthusiasm, jealousy, confidence, self-love, thoughts, imagination, mobilisation - all what that you want - whether it attracts you an upsurge in that which you admire, subsequently use this belief system, for today.

You do not need to telephone the facts, you are able to call it a real truth, a reality that in this time on your own life, currently, enables you to be of that which you would like to become. You don't have to become loyal to some paradigm, so you don't have to become loyal to a concept, a belief system, a notion, maybe not in all. There is a constant must swap your fullest well being for virtually any dedication. Perhaps not any single dedication in life is well worth exchanging your wellness for, for example devotion to a obsolete idea about god and that you will well be comparative to god.

The pupil version of divinity - at which divinity may be your teacher, life could be your faculty space, and you're the student - is of significance.

But humankind is nearing the close of the period where paradigm functions you.

Therefore, during biblical mindset someone might state that they will need to obtain exactly what purpose god has planned them (also it is irrelevant whether they state god, or even life, or even perhaps the universe, or even spirit it's the same), at the student mindset they'll state:"thati want to know about the courses i've came here to learn." both of the, to a level, are dis-empowering paradigms.

An invitation in to the partner paradigm

So we need to encourage one now, to start to tease, or even laugh, using a grand paradigm, the only one we predict that the co-creative or venture paradigm, at which you aren't living out an fate on the world is accountable, nor are you currently sitting on your lifetime for students, at-

tempting to make the right path through a program but as an alternative you - like us are an innovative force in life. No less valuable compared
to nonphysical companies you've got, however
only operating in an alternative measurement .

The measurement from that you run does not
necessarily signify your value into the machine .
You've guessed this all together. You've assumed
that since you exist at a compact measurement,
that must indicate that you're lower life-force
than such as those people who exist out that measurement by a brief margin. It's perhaps not too.
You've got various abilities out of us, however,
they're considerably lesser. You've got another
role out of us, however it's perhaps not lower.

You're very welcome to deny this truth if it's not
decent for you personally. Do not deny it ideo-

logically, deny it because its influence you is not a consequence you prefer .

But let us tell you some of those consequences of this co-creator paradigm. Inside this paradigm no bodysays:"thati want to locate my objective " they state:"thati desire to generate a objective. I would like to produce for myself a lifetime, that in accordance with me, offers great significance, and fantastic happiness, and about that i am very motivated." from the co-creator version there's the realization which my experience in my own life is vitally vital as what my entire life ends up being, or doing, or committing, or even achieving. There's the realization it is essential i ensure i'm motivated, i make certain i exist at precisely the way in which i want to exist. Therefore there's a great deal more responsibility within this paradigm than at another two in that is frequently the actual reason people reject it.

On the outside they refuse it as it sounds to position that individual beings could you need to be equal to spirit. But frequently the actual reason behind your rejection is as the consequences of the have become overwhelming comparative to the sort of liability and attractiveness and power and sway one carry. That you never all feel this, and also you don't all exercise , however you also do all take it. And this idea can be quite overwhelming.

If it's overwhelming, even if that really is not just a practical paradigm for you personally at this time, then it won't need a fantastic effect you. However, if it's a practical paradigm, then it is going to force you to feel free, a little giddy with freedom. This is likely to cause you to feel a bit nervous, as paradigmatic jumps do, however additionally, it will raise your awareness of fulfilment and mobilisation.

We find it equally funny and unhappy that people today become profoundly trapped, imprisoned, and with way of a belief of a objective. They articulate that until they see their own purpose that they cannot be happy. The thought of purpose is using an immobilising effect, a paralysing effect, but they use the thought. Even if this thought, this paradigm, isn't having a fantastic effect, it remains stuck to.

If there's 1 thing you take with you now, it can be this: do not let thoughts utilize you. You utilize thoughts. Therefore should they benefit you, use themwhatever belief, whatever the fact is fantastic for you personally to use ituntil it's no longer advantageous to youpersonally, then let yourself enlarge it.

You do not have to judge some thing in order to allow it move . We expect that you heard that. That you do not want to judge some thing to be able to allow it move. It is possible to just opt for an even far more expansive, or simply just of use, paradigm, occupation, belief system, whatever it can be. Due to the fact you let it go of just one thing doesn't suggest you are estimating it. It's possible for you to honor exactly what it's meant for you personally, you're able to honor that in one point its influence you had been good.

What we're talking about is based in the most deepest amount of belief, that will be all about that you're comparative to god. Simply take a look in exactly what beliefs, if unconscious or conscious, you've been applying relating to any of it. You've been using an opinion. It's not possible for somebody to not apply a notion about themselves in connection with divinity. Even when for them divinity does not exist, then there's still a romantic relationship. Thus take a gander at how you've been profoundly about divinity, also take a good peek at the effect it's in your own final decision making, in your own capacity to lifetime the complete, articles, excitingand balanced lifestyle. Then determine whether your grand paradigm will last better.

Loyalty has no location within a evolutionary system. We are aware that in some paradigms loyalty is very appreciated, exceptionally priced. However, if your attention is on your very own conscious development, loyalty isn't planning to be quite a practical feature in which to conduct your own life.

[assessing individuals in the area:] we're extremely pleased, even joyful, to put this . We haven't done it clearly and you've made this potential.

If you're from an puppet paradigm, or even perhaps a student paradigm, then that which we now have said would really feel erroneous as, at an student paradigm, so you ought to be here learning out of individuals who've superior wisdom as well as in an puppet paradigm, we all would be the individuals who've left all this possible any way, you're simply puppets. However, at a co-creative paradigm it's both us and you who've left this dialog potential . It's due to the insights that you have permitted in, on your preceding dialog a couple minutes ago, we can speak even as we did this. It's on account of the measures that you have obtained, the jumps you've left, the letting proceed you've enabled, which has made this specific dialog a possibility.

So know this really adventure here was created with both us and you. If it seems to be more useful, or intelligent, or shrewd, then realize those are features which are likewise part of you personally. Should you carry on to endeavor all of your favorable features on divinity you're likely to maintain your self at a level of development. We realize that it seems perhaps respectful and right to endeavor most your positive qualities on soul, however possess a careful look in exactly what the true effect of this can be on your true life.

That's how you judge your perception system. Perhaps not since it sounds fine, maybe not as it's now hot and exactly what every one is saying, maybe not as it seems to be both highminded and lofty but as a result of its actual result in the living of one's every day activity .So we will give you paradigm that's immensely respectful of you personally, and also in our opinion a good deal more mobilising compared to some of those paradigms you were accustomed to using. It isn't the previous model you're likely to strike , however for today it's a really valuable one online offer.

Current status: confusion and competing situations made by using different decisionmaking methods between your primary players at the inaugural conversion procedure.

Impact: decline in transformation synergy and rival transformation outcomes.

Desired endstate: facilitate a paradigm change with a consequent synergy of work between, and uniformity of, the more decision process of parties active in the conversion procedure.

Wallpaper: with conclusion of this assessment and entry of this report, there is a comprehensive review by the forces staff. Throughout their extensive inspection it became evident the forces team was fighting with all the tips contained in the organizational layouts exhibited within the analysis. The type of the questions which were asked and the clarifications necessary to be awarded signaled that the methodology used by the forces team to appraise the report differs from the methodology which has been used to build the report. Afterward, because we prepared for phaseii that may be the onset of implementation of these tips included and modified with inputs in headquarters staff, there again, did actually be both disconnects and misunderstandings to what had been essential to execute the arrangement advocated in the last report. The absence of settlement was vexing and it has contributed to a degree of frustration among parties involved. It seemed that the us team and the forces team weren't processing information exactly the exact same manner or employing precisely the very same decision manufacturing molds.

Diagnosis: tracking of this procedures used to test the submitted final report along with its guidelines, directed to this decision that an alternative decision paradigm has been used to assess and confirm the report and also the company essential for the conversion of their forces.

Decisionmaking paradigms possess evolved in substantially the exact same fashion as man has evolved. For nearly all of man's history that the decision-making-paradigm was founded in an agrarian society. The society established its conclusions on nature. Planting and harvesting has been founded upon the seasons and the current weather. First and foremost the life's conclusions were predicated on what's happening around these on a daily, season annually.

The basic ingredient being that the man or beast-of-burden has been the way to obtain work.

The introduction of the industrial revolution and also the construction and also debut of complex and contemporary machines demanded a fresh means of earning decisions. The decision paradigm shifted, replacement man since the way to obtain job, by machines. The system or mechanical-decision-paradigm rests upon three fundamental notions, which can be reductionism, investigation predicated on reductionism, and mechanics.

The very first of those thoughts is reductionism, that is situated on the premise that every thing we experience, perceive, touch, texture, or even handle is some thing that's composed of parts. Those pieces are wholes, which can be further constructed of parts. Therefore one of those essential questions to the machine-paradigm addresses would be your ultimate limitation of carrying things aside, as it had been an era that was obsessed with carrying things apart. This paradigm rests upon the easy belief that how to style or mend something would be to split this up into its unique bits, optimizing the person bits, reassemble themthereby, developing a small ideal machine. Therefore the first consolidating notion of this machine era was that what contains parts, and also so as to bargain with the item, you must simply take it apart, before eventually you reach ultimate pieces. Further, we should take action, because"x" is adequate for"y" - in case"x" does occur afterward"y" needs that occurs. This mechanical-decision-paradigm tries to build up a thought of earth in which everything are linked with sufficient and necessary relationship, of effect and cause. It's two important impacts. To begin with, is that after we decide to try to spell out some thing, call it"y" and then we detect its own origin,"x", we usually do not require anything else to describe it, as the justification is complete. When"x" is sufficient and necessary to create"y", then nothing matters. Secondly, this perspective of earth finishes everything is system; thus, every thing can be examined by breaking it down to its parts.

The next basic idea was that nearly all with the manner of thinking can be an activity called investigation. Diagnosis is only predicated on reductionism. The debate is for those who have what that you wish to explain, or even perhaps a challenge that you wish to solve, you begin to go apart. Which means you divide this up into its own components and you receive everything of the way down into the"ultimate" components, but you put down it as simple components while you can. You then explain the components or you also solve these issues so when you've them resolved or clarified, you aggregate those explanations or solutions to an answer or excuse for a complete. S o analysis is just a sort of"downup again" believing. It has an inclination to spell out things by the behaviour of their own parts.

Inside this decision paradigm in which a individual is faced with a issue, " he undergo an activity that's technically known from the jargon of direction ,"cutting it down to size". Cutting the issue down to size is only fixing it analytically. It is lowering it to some of solvable issues, solving both the component issues and assembling them in an answer for a whole. Because of this inside this paradigm, investigation became the most dominant mode of consideration; in reality, today we utilize analysis and believing concerning interchangeable terms. It's quite tricky for several folks to conceive of a alternate method of understanding authentic diagnosis.

The 3rd fundamental notion of this machine-decision-paradigm could be your concept from the name of this era derives, the notion is referred to as snowball. Psychotherapy relies upon the idea that most happenings on earth might be explained by consenting to merely a single relationship, which of cause and effect. The sort of the decision paradigm has been ordered by the use of these 3 thoughts into this practice of work. This chiefly taken care of the processor even the replacement of person as the way to obtain job, with an system. However work has been thought as the conversion of thing in 1 form to the conversion of energy and matter, or even the conversion of energy to one form or the other. To put it differently, work has been imagined physical provisions and, for that reason, mechanization was going to using machines to successfully carry out physical work. Man has been substituted as the way to obtain energy from machines. And how he had been replaced has been that the consequence of an atomistic manner we test work. The meeting line, the bulk production lineup, has been the epitome with in this manner of believing. However there are numerous significant impacts of this. As we identify these aspects of job, we experimented with mechanize themand also we did mechanize a few. There were a few that individuals did not have the relevant skills to accomplish, atleast initially, thus we put men to focus with those tasks with an essential outcome. We developed man-machine techniques, like doing physical work where the job had been conceptualized in such ways as to ease mechanization, and consequently, we put person to carrying out job which has been designed for/or such as a system.

Have you ever wondered why you afternoon you could be glad and a day later left feeling down and out? What causes stress and anxiety to creep in to your own life? This report examines the reason and consequence of one's regular modern realities and everything may possibly have shifted on your consciousness to create you feel tired, time inferior as well as maybe even emotionally drained. The majority folks understand right since it's our thoughts that make our activities.

That's just the entire world keeps shifting. Even though your world might not be just like every one else but this guide may assist you to weave your way from this paradigms, which might no longer function you. Such as a mental gps, then it is going to point your believing therefore can realize the journey ahead with some kind of calmness and hope to future years.

For the past thousands of years people happen to be utilizing the very same templates for producing distinct brands of the reality. 'That is how my pappy was able to accomplish it and that's the manner i'll take action, and also how i expect one to accomplish it' "you did it first, therefore i am gonnadoit straight back now!" i recall watching a episode of the sopranos where tony soprano cried into his loved ones,"outthere it may possibly be 2010, in here it 1958!" there you've got it in a nutshell. Anything that conditioning is holding back you continues to be lent for youpersonally, and you also openly made it and may possibly be affected the results. What psychological or programming pc software continues to be conducting your necktop computer? Usually, conflict arises as soon as the existing psychological picture clashes having a fresh sort of reality which sounds unacceptable and foreign. This will usually make it tough to maneuver forward specially when the brand new awareness thrusts you in the unknown. Stress can be due to a paradigm shift.

Most of us need things to remain exactly the same as it makes us feel much safer, safer and secure. Change by itself disturbs a whole lot of folks why change things once the old way worked fine? As the lake that's been flowing exactly the exact same means for a long time really isn't the exact same lake .Every thing changes, and it changes moment by moment. It's maybe not the exact same now river that flowed beyond here . Each living time brings for you a fresh circumstance, distinct factors and another probabilities. That is universal law enforcement and the sooner you accept this rule, the earlier you will grow more 'in song' together with your lifetime. The single constant in the world would be shift .

Some individuals have a collection perspective of the way that things ought to be. From the a few of my old schoolmates telling me he'd to eventually become a medical physician because that's exactly what his father expected . I watched him fight for decades and it wasn't his thing. He dropped short and settled to become a dental practitioner. I met him and found him to become a rather miserable person and that i really don't think he awakened once. Noone was dwelling and also the light was absolutely not on. Perhaps he'd have been better had he paid attention to their inner desires - that the people that typically originate from one's center. What limits will be stopping you from dancing? Can it be your own personal panic, or some body else? Paradigms usually come packed with restrictions and limitations and also you will need to become strong enough to break with their heritage or habits that keeps them set up.

Paradigms are thoughts, principles and legislation of behavior imposed upon uswith or without our approval. They dictate how people have to act and also impact our thinking into the idea whereby we wind up thinking what every one is thinks, simply to match. Expectation can put us up for disappointment as it creates hard-walled paradigms with minimal room for shift or chance of investigating the alternatives. Regrettably, some paradigms maintain us boxed-in and limit our perspective of this facts that might exist only beyond the carton. This could make it difficult regarding things for what they are really. Perception is ninetyfive percentage of reality, which could change from one individual to another.

The best method of understanding when a paradigm is damaging you're by estimating the way you're feeling at the current moment. Note the way the system responds. Can you really feel pain, are you currently experiencing awkwardness? Are you really excited, elated and onto a top? That really is the manual for which road to shoot at your fork. The man who goes ahead with finish abandon and surrenders thinking it could be the most effective that you may do at this time without any any negativity may be your person who finds better and newer manners for performing matters. If you anticipate negativity you're certain to think it is. Expect the opposite and you'll realize that, too!

Help To Learn How to Overcome Anxiety: What to consider

Anxiety is basic when we experience changes or advances in our lives. It is frequently connected to pressure, which is one of the numerous triggers of anxiety. Anxiety can influence us both emotionally and physically. Anxiety indications incorporate muscle strain, fractiousness, sentiments of stress, apprehension, or dread, dashing contemplations (for example your mind going a million miles per moment), and perspiring. Anxiety is a typical inclination and reaction. Albeit numerous individuals accept anxiety is an indication of shortcoming, those sentiments are basic for anybody confronting a basic change or emergency.

Anxiety can be overseen in a few unique ways. Rehearsing profound breathing activities is one, basic method for overseeing anxiety indications. In the midst of emergency, our anxiety is triggered and our psyches and bodies will in general be on "over-burden." Calm breathing is fundamental since it helps with hindering your breathing, enabling your body to arrive at a quiet state. It is essential to require some investment to simply sit and relax. With those living occupied lives, it can appear to be difficult to discover an opportunity to unwind and relax. Be that as it may, with the snappy exercise portrayed beneath, you can rehearse anyplace and all over the place!

Before rehearsing this procedure, I suggest you prepare your psyche and body. For instance, finding a tranquil spot can be useful. In some cases, shutting your eyes is useful also. The accompanying strategy is classified "quiet relaxing."

Some basic advances you can rehearse when you experience anxiety indications:

1. Take a moderate breath in through the nose, breathing into your lower stomach (for around 4 seconds).

2. Hold your breath for 1 or 2 seconds.

3. Exhale gradually through the mouth (for around 4 seconds).

4. Wait a couple of moments before taking another breath.

Taking 5 minutes to rehearse this day by day can be helpful. When you feel great with this system, you can build an opportunity to as long as 10 minutes. You can likewise join mind visuals. For instance, while rehearsing this system, you can close your eyes and picture something that quiets you (for example the sea or a knoll).

While this procedure can be useful, it is prudent to look for expert assistance should you feel your anxiety side effects compound after some time or seriously influence day by day exercises, for example, school and work. Should you believe you are looked with the more articulated impacts of anxiety, I find that having a sheltered domain to discuss your anxiety and what triggers it is significant (for example singular psychotherapy). Treatment can give a situation where you can investigate side effects and how it influences your psyche, body, and day by day associations. In treatment, you can talk about further approaches to deal with your side effects of anxiety.

The Natural Means for Overcoming Anxiety Disorder Panic Attacks

There is some uplifting news for those experiencing panic attacks in light of the fact that separated from the way that it is conceivable to defeat your anxiety disorder panic attacks, it is likewise conceivable to abstain from having them inside and out. The seriousness of the assault decides the sort of treatment that must be directed. Individuals who have been presented to the normal methods for managing this issue are so anxious to gain proficiency with the way toward counteracting it due to the horrendous experience they have experienced.

The vast majority of the individuals that experience the ill effects of assault are exhorted and urged to utilize recommend medications to thump themselves into an incapacitated state of mind where they won't experience panic assault or feelings by any means. On the off chance that you have been informed by individuals on the utilization with respect to medicine I think the inquiry you have to pose to yourself is, to what extent will you keep on relying upon medications for, to fix the assault; will you need to rely upon medications for an amazing remainder?

In the event that your answer is no, at that point, the normal methods for managing anxiety disorder panic assault is for you in light of the fact that basically what you are stating is medications won't fix your panic assault, other than the negative impact of medications can be decimating. Indeed, even Doctors are starting to concede that there are better methods for managing panic assault other than depending on meds constantly, an excess of medications could prompt dangerous circumstances. There are different types of treatment that individuals who are sick of taking drug can hold onto, for example, nourishing the brain all the time with positive messages.

Regular methods for adapting to the assault are sans medication, tranquilizes in some cases make the mind dull to help manage the assault yet the treatment will assist the cerebrum with recognizing when the assault are going to occur so you can maintain a strategic distance from them, worries of cutting edge living are triggers that causes assault, individual treatment will distinguish and defend triggers and you will get to a point where you can deal with feelings and anxiety in a develop style.

The best thing about regular methods for taking care of anxiety disorder is ones you vanquish certain dread it fabricates certainty towards the following case contrast with medications that manages the present dread and after that when something different happens you need to take another arrangements of medications to manage it. Individuals who use treatment deal with their nerves and will recover their trust in a matter of moments once they are prepared to experience the means at their own pace by discovering what works for them. Regardless of how exceptional the inclination is once you get into a typical routine it may involve time before you are thoroughly convey from the hooks of panic assault.

Out of the approaches to diminish anxiety attacks, the most ideal ways are to learn and ace the strategies to conquer it. It is one of only a handful couple of thoughts to diminish your anxiety assault. Somebody that has for once or more than once experienced panic assault and the misery that goes with it might perceive the state of alarm. Cling to the aides underneath and you will have the option to battle your anxiety assault at whatever point it is going to strike you.

Perceive that it is an anxiety assault

When you have perceived that you are going to encounter an anxiety assault, bit by bit loosen up yourself down and reflect about it reasonably, along these lines it will go behind you. Somebody that encounters anxiety assault know without a doubt that its inclination shows up and vanishes. Whenever you experience anxiety assault, accept it as something that is genuine and furthermore remember that will leave with time. Perceiving that you are experiencing an assault is the primary measure to diminishing it.

Perform stuffs that are named physical

Attempt to play out certain exercises, sit in front of the television or perform something that is probably going to remove your brain from the assault. A few people guarantee that just by doing practices they can get their psyche off the disorder. Doing exercises that are known to be physical releases endorphins, knocking up your outlook. You can too utilize it to leave pressure, which are typically the known reason for anxiety attacks. Try not to act feeble, help yourself by performing stuffs that are viewed as physical, the more productive the best for you.

Connect with your companion gathering

Connect with your buddies and relations that think about the thing you are experiencing. It is an endeavor to contact your encouraging group of people to get empathy, however it is an open door for your buddies and relations to help you at the time you require it critically. You can perform comparative stuff for them later on, yet right then and there give them access to help you. This will diminish the anxiety attacks.

A few people are bashful that they typically appear to be on edge and keep up it as a mystery, particularly from buddies and relations. This is just going to increase the entire circumstance and you won't perceive any individual to converse with when you require it. I let you know, on the off chance that you let go of the circumstance you are covering from your buddies, you would be astounded to see that you are not by any means the only individuals that experience such attacks. As a general rule, a mess of individuals have experienced some sort of anxiety or panic disorder once or more than that in their reality. When you understand that you have anxiety assault, experience what it has an aftertaste like and the way that it can pass by you, you will wind up supporting yourself to manage the feelings of a panic disorder.

All in all, how would you treat anxiety and stress? All things considered, it's hard to pinpoint one explicit solution for anxiety, yet with a little mental fortitude and a decent procedure, you can figure out how to defeat your fears. How about we begin.

Most importantly, if your anxiety is overpowering to the point that it's keeping you from carrying on with your life, at that point you have to change your way of life. If so, there are three fundamental parts of your life that you should look at and after that make the vital changes. They are as per the following: your physical action, your eating routine, and how you rest.

Exercise to Relieve Anxiety

It's constantly critical to work out; nonetheless, on the off chance that you are a restless individual, at that point exercise is fundamental. Practicing does numerous things. It drives out poisons made by anxiety, it changes your general outlook, and it just makes you feel much improved.

In the event that you right now work out, at that point you definitely know the constructive outcomes it can have at the forefront of your thoughts and body. For every other person, you have to begin practicing immediately, with the goal that you can get yourself into a daily practice.

From the start, do what is agreeable (to avoid damage) however consistently attempt to augment your exertion so you get a total exercise. The principal month and half ought to be tied in with making a daily schedule and fortifying your muscles for perseverance and finesse. Make a point to get a smidgen of cardio with the goal that you can actually work out the poisons made by dread and anxiety. You can likewise perform different weight opposition activities, for example, weight lifting or utilizing obstruction groups. The greatest thing to recall is to set the bar ever more elevated with the goal that you can amplify your endeavors.

Trust me, on the off chance that you build up an everyday practice, your anxiety will diminish and you'll likewise look better all the while! It may not be a sensational change, however you'll begin to feel increasingly great about yourself and you'll really begin to think in an unexpected way. For me, practice turned into a discharge and I found that I could work out a portion of my issues during my exercise routine. Anyway, what are you sitting tight for? Go!

Diet to Help Anxiety Relief

Another significant viewpoint that you have to consider to treat anxiety is watching what you eat. Once more, slimming down is significant for your wellbeing notwithstanding in the event that you have anxiety disorder or not, however on the off chance that you are experiencing anxiety certain diet can either trigger your tensions or help you feel much improved.

Okay, so where do you start? You have to eat a well-adjusted eating routine. Obviously, that is the thing that each master says. What does a well-adjusted eating regimen involve? First off, quit going out to eat and shop at a market. When you got out, odds are you don't know precisely what's in the nourishment and you're presumably eating oily sustenance with high fats, which are on the whole horrendous for anxiety. When shopping in a market, shop in the border and attempt to stay away from the inside isles. The items sold in the inside piece of the store for the most part contain a poo heap of additives that neutralize your anxiety.

When shopping in the border, go for produce, for example, products of the soil, get other sound foods like fish, normal nuts, and even eggs, and you limit your dairy admission. Additionally, as an update, you should investigate the fixings on everything and recollect that the less fixings contained in the item, the better.

Chapter Four

Rewire negative thoughts into positive

Hen many folks hear the expression positive awareness, they'll call it positive believing or they'll consider a particular topic to raise awareness for, such as aids or diabetes and maybe themes such as the surroundings. Favorable awareness is getting to be a brand new standalone term that shows we have been conscious of the ramifications which our favorable energy continues on our world, in addition to on every one life.

Many folks produce positive energy sporadically instead of always, therefore its effects have become shortterm. The energy that is generated can be quite good in its debut, however the moment it turns out to the earth, it can dissipate or become diluted with each the destructive energy which exists in this distance.

In case you were to make a continuous flow of energy that is positive, not merely in every time of one's daily life, but when you dream, you'd become an extremely positive force on your distance. Your distance would also enlarge as the vitality within it expands, so making your world grow larger withit. With time, your field of favorable energy can be so huge itwont permit any unwanted energy to go into.

Negative energy is created in various forms by unwanted people and additionally jaded by them. Examples of these would be the items you imagine, the more things you state, exactly what you have confidence in or place your faith or confidence in, and also your own emotional condition. Because this detrimental energy develops in a individual's space, it brings a lot more of the exact same energy for this. No sum of positive projections will ruin that unwanted energy, since the favorable energy that is generated is instantly removed by the damaging energy which exists for you.

Many individuals are constantly moving out of 1 end of this energy scale into one contrary, developing a random mixture of favorable and negative energies which offset out each other out, leaving just a little investment supporting, either negative or positive, but not enough of one to make difference.

The strongest positive energy which you're able to cause is by simply using just positive thoughts, by speaking in mere favorable provisions, by putting your confidence in mere things that last and by keeping up a joyful psychological condition. While that is great in theory, let us be fair. Just how a lot of folks are able to say they think just positive thoughts, speak only in favorable conditions, put their beliefs only favorable things and keep up a joyful emotional-state 99.9percent of their time? Not too many, however, the wonderful idea about the technique i use is that it allows room for mistakes and provides you with the possibility to fix these.

Thus, in other words, even for those who have a negative idea or produce a negative announcement, you get the chance to change it out by re thinking it restating it in a certain manner, using just words that are positive. All words that are negative in their should really be avoided. This guarantees that most negativity is expunged and also you merely make energy. Putting your beliefs, beliefs and trust in to just positive things might become of a struggle for you personally and keeping up a joyful psychological state might also. However, so long as you're actively changing just as much depreciation to favorable as possible, you can earn a good change in your own energy field.

Now you know how to help it become happen, why should it matter anyway? If you're sharp, you found the solution to this question. Whenever you're negative, you then bring negativity. This really is that simple. Like-energies draw eachother and unlike tails offset outside.

That which is made from energy, vibrating at various prices and the ones different speeds determine negative or positive, particularly with thoughts. Your thinking are everywhere where your creative process begins to grow. A tree vibrates a fantastic bit more slowly than the usual head do, but it does not signify that the shrub is negative. What's relative to another person. It'd be the like comparing apples into baseballs. While they have been a world, that is about the one thing they have in common, apart from which they may also be both made from energy.

When it comes to getting what exactly you desire in life, using just favorable energy means that you obtain just positive things coming for you. This usually means that unwanted important things in life are no more drawn to you. Additionally, it usually means that process of eliminating negativity is finally going to cause the human brain to rewire itself due of this re-programming you have obtained it all through. You're going to be astounded at what goes on in the event that you realize a negative results to a upcoming situation. The human mind knows that negativity is usually to be avoided, therefore it alters the specific situation to some thing favorable for you personally. That is what's been happening for me personally also it makes me grin each moment.

There's yet another part to the i want to indicate for your requirements. Weather systems are positive or negative energy, as an instance, higher pressure or reduced pressure. A bright sunny day with very low humidity is elevated pressure or energy. A type of intense thunderstorms with tornadoes is an incredibly strong damaging energy section. Your negativity may draw in these storms directly into a door or your positivity can dissolve them make them move everywhere. I've undergone this and continue to think it is to become true.

Ofcourse there are plenty of small hints which might be of enormous help as you're with this course for you seeing real consequences. And the procedure isn't likely to occur over night, as every destructive thought and every unfavorable announcement that you have said or had has come to be a habit with you personally and also the human mind is wired like that. The only real means that you're going to improve it out really is by always creating just favorable energy. And because favourable energy grows larger and more complicated, it is going to rewire the human brain to make just positive energy that you by altering any perceived unwanted effect to something favorable.

So that you have it. I hope that you will require through this procedure instead of simply find so many amazing and new positive chances introducing themselves for youpersonally, but since you shift, the planet changes together with you in favorable ways. In the course of time, you're going to have the ability to manifest your fantasy. Please see our web logs on blogger,"journey to favorable awareness" and"the power of positive awareness" for plenty of great suggestions about making this process easier, in addition to benefits of experiencing favorable awareness.

The way your past programs the human brain

There are not many people who will declare we've come out of the youth unscathed or possess had fairy-tale relationships. We've had a few very awful things happen to people. A lot worse than the others. Too frequently though we play those negative thoughts repeatedly till they truly are part of our complete mental makeup. Whatever you do would be directed by the way you view your own past.

Think that it's not correct? If you are always fighting with money, weight, or love... That really is a crystal clear sign your past is at the driver's seat!

Want more proof? Think about a fantasy you have. This really is moving straight back to school, getting off from mr./ms. Wrong, or even finally leaving this deadend job. What goes on when you imagine that? Matters appear throughout the spot to avoid you from dancing. You can not actually get beyond the idea procedure not to mention actually setting up an attempt to generate a healthier life.

Perhaps you feel fearful, unworthy, confused, stressed, and sometimes overly stressed. You think of plenty of explanations perhaps not to pursue enjoyment. That is your past restraining you. That is most the negative, screwed-up people you struck all through your lifetime who had a hand in recruiting your own mind.

Exercise: re-programming your sub-conscious

Below, right now, deny to reside in your own negative thoughts more. All it functions would be to create your energy down level and encircle you with a feeling that prevents such a thing besides coming back to your own life.

Inch. Whenever a negative idea concerning the last pops up emotionally yell the term"stop!" or envision a person blowing a whistleanything that may disrupt those wellworn nerve pathway grooves. Some timesi will sing a song just as loudly as i could either aloud or within my own mind.

Your goal here will be to consciously take charge of one's own subconscious.

2. When you've disrupted this. Thought patter, replace it with a favourable memory that is equally powerful. For example, say you're mistreated as a youngster and a certain event pops to mind. Rather than giving into the memory, then bring a joyful memory you've got and remember it at as much detail as feasible.

3. In case you have hardly any joyful memories, or even believe it is tough to think of some thing when anger or annoyance attack, produce a set of some joyous occasions if you are at a fantastic mood and browse this list whenever you are feeling down. Until i have better in re-routing my thoughts i'd read my list five days every day or longer.

4. You could even write down prospective events you would like to see. In the event that you were really poor connection, then write what you need on another relationship. (be honest though nobody's perfect!) Jot down exactly what your own prospective partner would soon be enjoy plus some joyful times you may love to share with you along with him/her. Additionally, this is a excellent solution to program the own mind and energy field to bringing everything you desire .

The last is gone, it is performed and over. The only way that you may have some effect you currently will be if you allow it to. People"bad memory" paths have worn a groove on mind, therefore it is a whole lot easier to remember themwhether people want it or maybe not. Elect to reprogram your mind and realize the big difference it makes on your mood, and also on your own life.

Positive affirmations are a strong method to re-program the subconscious mind from negative thinking to positive. The idea is to choose the words of exactly what anybody would love to see based within his lifetime, and replicate them so those are a part of the manner of believing and visiting that the world. The favorable affirmation workin ways those posses the unwanted selftalk. It can work. Additionally, it will also help replace the negative thought with all the potent optimistic thinking.

It's remarkably natural to demand your self with the unwanted things constantly that can be called negative selftalk. In the event that you may use the energy of positive affirmation and equipped to replicate it in your self, this ability will allow one to restrain the human mind. This attitude may change your believing structure at any circumstance and also the method of your own feel-ings.

Getting optimistic is unexpectedly beneficial. This item can help become stronger and boost your self esteem. This attitude will permit you to go a way from the adverse believing. Anybody who wished to improve life instantly should make use of the energy. Anybody can replace her or his unwelcome beliefs in to powerful beliefs by injuries thought procedure. It's obtainable. Could be some beliefs that are harmful are ruling your mind. It's extremely simple to modify the method to grow the circumstance. You only have to take actions to rehearsal just some positive affirma-tion over and over before develop a construc-tive or expedient habitual idea pattern. Getting the most of those approaches is at a no manner arduous task. It's an simple job of studying the affirmations. Should you read those loudly, the operation will probably increase. By using rules that are positive, anybody can exude positive ideas in with them with all the aim of attraction out the whole possibility of these favourable confirmation.

Cardiovascular framework reaction

Anxiety can make changes the pulse and the course of blood all through the body. A quicker pulse makes it simpler to escape or battle, while expanded blood stream carries new oxygen and supplements to the muscles. At the point when veins limited, this is called vasoconstriction, and it can influence body temperature. Individuals regularly experience hot flashes because of vasoconstriction.

Accordingly, the body sweats to chill off. This can once in a while be excessively compelling and make an individual vibe cold. Long haul anxiety may not be useful for the cardiovascular framework and heart wellbeing. Some studies suggest that anxiety builds the danger of heart sicknesses in generally solid individuals.

Weakened insusceptible capacity

For the time being, anxiety helps the safe framework's reactions. Be that as it may, delayed anxiety can have the contrary impact.

Cortisol counteracts the arrival of substances that reason aggravation, and it turns off parts of the resistant framework that battle contaminations, debilitating the body's regular invulnerable reaction. Individuals with chronic anxiety disorders might be bound to get the normal cool, this season's flu virus, and different types of disease.

Changes in stomach related capacity

Cortisol squares forms that the body considers superfluous in a battle or flight circumstance. One of these blocked procedures is absorption. Likewise, adrenaline diminishes blood stream and loosens up the stomach muscles. Accordingly, an individual with anxiety may encounter queasiness, the runs, and an inclination that the stomach is beating. They may likewise lose their hunger. Some exploration recommends that pressure and gloom are connected to a few stomach related infections, including touchy inside disorder (IBS).

One investigation, of outpatients at a gastroenterology center in Mumbai, revealed that 30–40 percent of members with IBS additionally had anxiety or melancholy.

Urinary reaction

Anxiety and stress can expand the need to pee, and this response is progressively basic in individuals with fears. The need to pee or lost power over pee may have a transformative premise, as it is simpler to escape with an unfilled bladder.

Stress & How it Affects Your Body And How To Prevent It - Stress Anxiety Management

Stress is something that nobody truly needs to manage or confront. As everybody knows, you should manage the circumstances sooner or later and time. Fleeing from your issues won't illuminate anything. In some cases, it exacerbates things and harder to manage. This is the point at which you need pressure anxiety the executive abilities.

There are actually no huge mysteries with regards to overseeing pressure. Simply various strategies and systems that may support you.

Each strategy won't work for everybody. You need to know your degree of stress and how you are at present managing it.

The absolute initial step to assuming responsibility for your circumstance is to unwind. Locate a pleasant calm spot to let free and unwind. Regardless of whether it's just for a couple of minutes. Set aside a few minutes to have some alone reflection time and let go of everything. This is clearly significantly more difficult than one might expect, yet you can do it. When you set out to something, complete it at that point. Try not to pause and hold things off. You are dragging out the circumstance and this occasionally exacerbates the situation.

Time the executives and being sorted out is something else that will help you in the realm of stress. In all honesty, this will likewise facilitate your brain. Individuals' homes and work-places frequently demonstrate an image of what's in somebody's brain. Take seven days to place things in their correct spot and clear your psyche as you do it. You'll be astonished at the amount more you can complete.

Acknowledgment is the subsequent stage. Face it, there are only a few things that you won't have the option to change. Regardless of the amount you need to, the appropriate response and circumstance will continue as before. Acknowledge these changes, adjust to them, and proceed onward. Figure out how to release things. When you figure out how to do this effectively, a lot of pressure will be lifted off of you.

Have a great time! Life isn't all silly buffoonery, however it's not all work and taking care of tabs. Go for a stroll, spend time with companions, make the most of your family, take end of the week excursions. You will be flabbergasted at how things change once you take in some outside air and get a difference in landscape.

Make a brief period consistently for you to accomplish something that you like. Play a game or go out to eat at your preferred eatery. It may not be a ton of time for you to do this, yet this tad of time is significant. Your body needs alleviation similarly just as your psyche.

It seems like it's more difficult than one might expect, however you should simply put your brain to it and remain centered. Try not to have something intended to do each day throughout the day. Resting is additionally a significant piece of discharging pressure. Kick back and watch a motion picture, read a book, or tune in to music. Plan something with the expectation of complimentary yourself and brain of upsetting circumstances for some time.

How can every daily life coming together? I am certain that, compared to this specific afternoon that the team of the apollo 13 needed since they were in the way home to world.

The return flight of apollo 13 will forever be among the very famous flights recorded ever. And what the majority of men and women remember most vividly is that the single comment:"houston, we've got an issue."

Today life, and everyday living in overall, is just a process, and also an ongoing set of chances. Several of those chances are pure pleasure and pleasure plus a few are of a nature which requires for another sort of flexibility, endurance and endurance. Even the apollo 13 team faced a struggle that threatened their own physical presence on a degree that will have conquered many humans, because most humans haven't heard to perfect their own emotions. What they will have heard, alternatively, is always to be directed by their own emotions, and that's just another way of being mastered by their own emotions.

If there's anything that illustrates the significance of controlling feelings, the yield trip of apollo 13 does this. Because, a lot more important compared to the thousand upon millions of dollars which have been at stake, human lives were at stake. The apollo crew attracted themselves dwelling safely, together with the assistance of this houston team, because they retained their minds, focused their heads conscious and unconscious levels and believed and listened effortlessly.

And you may be thinking, "exactly what exactly does that have to do with me personally?" i'm not even an astronaut, and never will be.

I'll keep coming back to this! Changing gears, i'm wondering if you saw the first set of"the apprentice"? If this is so, you realize who bill rancic is. He's usually the main one (out of 216,000 applicants) who eventually became trump's helper, against all likelihood. I heard bill talk lately and he clarified the challenges and experiences that they were placed through, for example lasting 1 2 weeks sleeping just 12 hours every night, literally forcing them into the border physically, emotionally and emotionally. Perhaps that partially clarified omarosa! In terms of bill ranciche revealed his power to perfect his own feelings instead of having his feelings master as most of the different candidates did.

Again, you may be thinking, "exactly what exactly does that have to do with me personally?" i am not going on"the apprentice." fair enough.

Yet daily, folks you understand, for example your self, encounter situations which involve assessing emotions, for psychological intelligence.

You may be a mother or dad-who at the last whilst at a store together with your youngster, appeared and... Your son or daughter was no where to be observed! What exactly was your reaction? Now you realize the significance of"controlling emotions!" and think about the faculty student moving in to your last exam that's crucial for her long run? Or look at a recent adventure of the oldest daughter, dana, that graduates from the loyola university/ chicago that june. She worked on an important newspaper, just to reduce it once her computer crashed. She had to compose the newspaper , using merely a number hours to re write it. And that's what she managed to complete, as sometime past she'd acquired the beliefs and skillsets involved with producing useful psychological and mental conditions needed for such scenarios. And well she had this particular talent, as in the start of her schedule, her class had been told that over a calendar year, just roughly 1 / 2 of those could be nursing students. The others could be pushed by the rigors of this app. Simply speaking they were told that those washing would not have the ability to deal with the"stress element."

Think about the individual being called to the supervisor's office, after many rounds of"down sizing?" and also the unexpected emergency room doctor being faced with all the worst instance she's seen, and significantly more than that, hasn't handled. . .knowing a lifetime is at her palms? Or even the spouse who's been informed with their own partner he or she no longer wants to keep in the union. And think about somebody in your office which you wouldn't wish on anybody? Some one who does exactly what they are able to on a normal basis to test to"push your buttons"

The truth is that in a continuing cornerstone, we're called on to answer situations, circumstances and people that involve psychological endurance, flexibility, attention, imagination, and also the capacity to continue to keep our minds, as we say.

Luckily, every person has an amazing chance to find out the art collections the faith, the principles, and also the behaviours that take part in the situation of"mastering emotions." with the term"controlling emotions," i'm speaking about mastering your emotions as well as the mental conditions and behaviours of the others around you. The others, for the large part, haven't learned the way to effortlessly make exactly what icall"of use conditions" to their own. I shall go as far as to state most humans are educated precious little about controlling emotions. . .about the way exactly they could comprehend and resourcefully respond for their emotions. . .and into the feelings of the other, their kids, their family members, their associates, their coworkers, their managers, managers or employees!

Normal and. ..unhealthy

Many folks that i speak to and socialize with have almost no understanding to how they're creating their very own emotional states within an continuing basis. I mean, many human beings think that what creates their psychological conditions is that the specific circumstance they are confronting, exactly what somebody else has said , or exactly what a few man did or failed to do since they socialized together. Moving farther, many folks would say it really is"ordinary" to answer"hard circumstances" with stress, anger, uncertainty, and in spite of some amount of"helplessness." isay,"twist ordinary " because that which i've found are tactics to respond efficiently and resourcefully from exactly what many state may not be reacted to resourcefully and efficiently! And did i really do that? By simply detecting the simple fact that the others have heard to accomplish that, and simply by requesting somebody who'd mastered exactly what i wished to master how to instruct and teach me howto accomplish exactly that!

In the end, i'd discovered to respond at a significantly less than resourceful means to many conditions of life. And i then heard that behavior is learned behaviour. Therefore, why not i find out how to perfect emotions? And that's what i chose to accomplish five decades back. This decision, and all that followedwas among the smartest decisions i'd made in my own life. Period.

I think that when we can't possess our own emotions and require whole responsibility for those emotions we make , it is going to be rather hard, maybe impossible, for all of us to generate the life we truly desire. Where's your wisdom of creating stress for ourselves and people around us at precisely the exact same time frees our efforts supporting our hopes and fantasies? And that's just what we can do if we trust circumstances and

others to create healthy and satisfying psychological conditions for ourselves!

Because, life goes just as we need, does one?
People are not even close to flawless, and we
never have seen a method yet to put ourselves
within a environment where all can be as we all
desire. That means you might choose a more"well
organized results," then go for it, as well as at
the procedure for one's travel, innumerable alterations are required! The others don't do as you'd
prefer to allow them to accomplish, or simply the
elements isn't perfect for what you're opting for.
For example, my daughter jamie, who's at spain
studying for your session had proposed a weekend at the hills recently and has been excited
about her plans into being at the snowcapped
sierra nevada mountains. Nevertheless, the afternoon before she had been to venture up the

mountain, it snowed, and snowed, and snowed, and snowed, and snowed more! The mountain peaks had been also inaccessible by car. . .and she left alterations to her plans therefore she'd like her weekend. Now, just how a lot of do you know who stop on a break simply to whine about that or this. . .because matters do not fit up with your own expectations and requirements?!

The annals of life...

Are up for you

Consider the countless millions of humans that wakeup on an everyday basis to"face daily," and do this by significantly less than zest, energy and passion for that which they'll do daily.

Is life not overly short, and also prized to live like that? Is life important enough for all of us to really know, " i am really learn, the way to generate a rich and resourceful inner lifestyle, and a pair of beliefs, values and behaviours which let us proceed throughout your afternoon, the week, and the month, and so to talk with a resourcefulness and flexibility to generate the feelings we want to have, as opposed to being victims to context or into other individual beings?

Seeing"mastering emotions," you will find skills which we are able to know, like how to build exactly what i call a"foundation state," that will be rather straightforward and gratifying to master with some guidance, even within the telephone. It's possible to discover to alter certain beliefs through a fitness called"the belief change exercise!" or you may discover how to readily, and yes after all readily, respond"neutrally" to an earlier event that at days gone by was quite painful for you personally when you recalled it. Whenever you find out to make use of the human mind in an alternative way, each one these things are absolutely straightforward. Fixing phobias, eliminating stress, sadness or stress. There'll be ample folks telling us just how hard it's to complete exactly what i've just clarified. They're secured in precisely the exact same mindset of people that only knew that person flight via an air craft wasn't potential, and it would not be potential for noise traveling through cables, or computers could not be small or cheap enough to the masses. Thus, believe what you may. Personally personally, i would prefer to follow somebody who's performing exactly what every one says may be carried out!

To learn feelings and also be joyful is the dream of each individual. Emotions would be the energized feelings. Someone can't avoid feelings because it that the spontaneous reaction to situation. Collars come with a large array of sense like guilt, anxiety, anger, and unworthiness. Any how, emotions can hamper the enjoyment of a individual, once the individual becomes influenced in the deluge of emotions. To keep a joyful prognosis, it has come to be an essentiality to restrain the emotions.

Emotions become dangerous, when it impacts the individuals, getting together with you personally. It's common that from the cases of emotion that is uncontrolled, it impacts outraged behavior and could hurt others feeling. Ergo feelings certainly really are a sequential activity, which in place, can severely affect the whole society. The real history of humanity shows that a number of the black marks happened for just one psychological out fracture of the individual. The control over emotions is vital, too because, it is going to help one better mold as a fantastic humans.

As explained, avoidance of feelings will be not functional from the everyday lifetime; a individual can simply restrain the emotions. The very first rung on the ladder to restrain the emotions is to begin with from the understanding of these emotions. You've got to first make your mind up to restrain the emotions. Bear in mind, emotions eventually become dangerous, whenever you respond to your urge. The simple point to be cautious would be to block your response. The replicated idea method and regular awarding will limit your outspoken character. But be mindful and seek the recommendations of the pros while becoming started as the reduction of these feelings can cause any different sort of disturbances. It's likewise a good idea to a main identification about the behaviour of this individual since in many circumstances, the mental out fractures are due because of emotional disorders.

The custom of psychological comfort methods is the perfect means to restrain the emotions. The comfort methods like yoga, meditation, bio feedback and forth innovative remedies can assist you unwind your brain and maintain mind, on mind. Religious faith is additionally major aspect that could offer you consciousness. Involvement on your favourite arts and sports can be also a favorite method, that'll relax both body and mind. Some current studies reveal that diet plays a part in the workout fractures and thus, you ergo you've got to exercise a balance dietplan. The step-by-step self-control exercise is focused on remold the men for an issue free and joyful life.

Being joyful is your aim of everybody. For this, remember an old expression, so, in the event you would like to be joyful, keep the others contented. Thus, stop for an instant, whenever you be in contact something which increases your own emotions. Just take a deep breath and consider the particulars of the matter. It's sure , when you are able to spare a minute to re think, it is possible to absolutely advance to assessing your feelings and become an extremely delighted individual.

Many of us who would like to shed weight already know just what they will need to complete. Simply, exercise and eat more. Okay i admit it is slightly bit more complicated than that, but frankly perhaps not just a whole lot! I accept it is critical to consume healthy wholesome foods, so reduce the total amount of fat dense, nutrient poor junk-food and stick to a suitable exercise regimen predicated on our unique requirements. But i endure within my first contention that the majority of people now know very well what they have to complete in order to reach their desirable weight and body form.

Why do we always keep asking the incorrect question,"just how do i lose fat " a hunt on am azon.co.uk indicates there are now 4,494 books coping in various manners for this vexing question. By always trying to find an solution for the question we state ourselves to thinking that individuals don't understand, consequently we don't ask more of use questions which may provide more insight and also help us in our pursuit for a thinner body. I feel a more useful question could be"why do i drink and eat more than i desire "

Nature's method of allowing us understand we are in need of food is appetite. Nevertheless, in advanced society people utilize food in various ways outside our physiological requirements. As an instance food may be the attention of several social activities and family events and all these should enjoy and appreciated. The actual problem is that when we utilize food in a effort to handle uncomfortable emotions and feelings. We're conditioned out of our earliest youth to make use of food as a distracter. When baby cries mother assesses the toddler, whether it's okay then baby gets' a jar or perhaps a soother so we know that food can be really a means to flee, even from an embarrassing sense. Emotional ingestion compels us to overeat with no idea or logical control.

It defies all logic, also following eating a meal that is satisfying you are able to undergo a ravenous appetite to have certain foods. Sadly we very rarely wish to overeat on celery or lettuce, no people crave that the thick, salty fat laden meals which are bombarded with carbs but possess little if any vitamins and minerals. What's more, no quantity of food may meet the emotion that is uncomfortable, in reality the moment we've swallowed the cake or chocolate that the atmosphere returns again however this time it's a whole lot worse because we all feel guilty. This puts into motion a binging cycle which may drive us into the verge of grief.

Emotional eating is a unconscious reaction. At one level i'm aware i wish to eat healthily and lose some unwanted pounds but i can't help myself and i'm attracted towards the cupboards in a vain effort to feel much better.

If we are able to master psychological ingestion and just eat response to authentic physiological appetite afterward i really feel that weight reduction could be easier and also our results much more notable. Together with proper workout weight loss could be permanent and also our health vastly enhanced. Emotional eating can be quite efficiently addressed through hypnosis. Successful weight loss is just continual in case your subconscious thoughts is re educated and favorable healthful customs are developed leading to varied attitudes towards food. The actual secret is in utilizing acupuncture to take care of the uncomfortable feelings and the emotions which drive them. Breaking this habit of ingestion in reaction to psychological causes makes weight loss a lot simpler and takes off the thought of always fighting to reach fat loss.

Chapter Five

Avoid anxiety and stress

Managing stress and anxiety may be finished with the ideal advice accessible. Stress and stress affects individuals in many walks of life. You that are one of many who believe isolated. Have a look at forums and community classes where you will discover countless people that are afflicted as you're. It will not also need to be considered a losing struggle and you can find means so as to handle this painful issue. Medications and drugs are readily available to help combat it we must prefer the non-toxic and natural remedies in managing tension and stress.

Decide on a period where you can fulfill and day your pals. Talking and sharing about your issues using them may diminish your stress levels immediately. Requesting sound advice can offer you with various options about what best to manage stressful conditions.

Schedule off a time out of the hectic day and focus on pampering your self. Treat your self into a nice hot bubble bath, go running, buy or simply relax with a fantastic novel. Tasks such as these may simply take away your mind from the everyday pressures and anxieties.

Stress and anxiety is generally brought around by life's failures and disappointments. Our aims in life help us focus and establishing attainable goals will encourage us in getting what you would like to realize. Setting small goals bring us nearer to that particular one huge goal, 1 step at the same time. It is going to surely offer a enormous ego boost and function as a trust builder every single time we reach our objectives. We'll soon be equipped in managing stress and anxiety.

You may want to try out writing in a journal. Many men and women find it therapeutic to write their thoughts down and feelings. You can be more aware of the things which cause one to be stressed and stressed. You can avoid those scenarios as you have identified them or you might be prepared to take care of situation since they happen appropriately.

What is it about anxiety that is terrible to the point that generally advanced individuals are rushed to escape it? The impressions of fate or fear or panic felt by sufferers are genuinely overpowering - the extremely same sensations, actually, that an individual would feel if the most noticeably terrible truly were going on. Over and over again, these, actually, fear full, sickening sensations drive customers to the moment help of drug, which is promptly accessible and considered by numerous insurance agencies to be the main line of treatment. Also, what great specialist would propose skirting the prescriptions when an enduring patient can get symptomatic help rapidly?

In any case, what customers don't have the foggiest idea when they start taking prescriptions is the unacknowledged expense of depending exclusively on pills: they'll never get familiar with some essential techniques that can control or dispose of their manifestations without drugs. They never build up the apparatuses for dealing with the anxiety that, more then likely, will turn up again at whatever point they feel undue pressure or experience critical life changes. What they ought to be told is that the correct psychotherapy, which instructs them to control their own anxiety, will offer help from anxiety in only weeks- - about a similar measure of time it takes for a SSRI to end up compelling.

Obviously, specialists realize that disposing of symptomatology isn't equivalent to wiping out etiology. Basic mental causes or triggers for anxiety, for example, those originating from injury, aren't the objective of the executives systems; they require longer-term psychotherapy. Be that as it may, anxiety - the executive procedures can offer alleviation, and offer it expediently.

The disagreeable indications well on the way to be helped by prescription are the extremely ones that the 10 best-ever anxiety-the executives pro-cedures are expected to address. They fall into three commonplace groups:

The physical excitement that establishes the dread of panic;

The "wired" sentiments of strain that corre-spond with being "worried" and can incorporate pit-of-the-stomach fate;

The psychological anguish of rumination- - a mind that won't quit thinking upsetting musings.

An advisor outfitted with strategies for tending to these groups can offer her restless customer the guarantee of alleviation for a lifetime, on the off chance that she knows which of these "10 best" methods work for which indications, and how to utilize them.

Group One: Distressing Physical Arousal

Panic is the physical excitement that sends numerous customers running for Xanax. Thoughtful excitement causes the heart-pounding, beat dashing, bleary eyed, tingly, brevity of-breath physical side effects that can emerge out of out of nowhere, and are painful when not comprehended. Indeed, even elevated amounts of intense anxiety that aren't as extreme as by and large panic attacks can comprise exceptionally agonizing states of excitement. Physical manifestations of anxiety incorporate steady increased physical strain in the jaw, neck, and back, just as an emotional-substantial sentiment of fate or fear in the pit of the stomach. The sentiment of fate will constantly set off a psychological quest for what may cause it.

Awful as these side effects may be, there are techniques that, when pursued normally as long lasting propensities, offer enormous alleviation.

Technique 1: Manage the Body.

Advising anxiety-inclined customers to deal with their bodies by eating right, keeping away from liquor, nicotine, sugar, and caffeine, and practicing is a strikingly standard "medicine," however not doing these things can undermine the adequacy of other antianxiety systems. Throughout the late spring before Ellie headed out to school, for instance, she'd nearly disposed of her anxiety by rehearsing profound, quiet breathing and figuring out how to stop her cataclysmic reasoning. She'd even had the option to quit taking the antianxiety drug she'd utilized for a considerable length of time. In any case, two months in the wake of beginning school, her panic attacks returned thundering furiously. She returned to see me, however rapidly let me realize that she was going to call her specialist for another Xanax solution. I recommended that, before she decided, she put in half a month keeping a "panic profile"-- a diary recording when and under what conditions she experienced panic attacks.

Half a month later, she went to my office grinning comprehensively. "I made sense of it," she stated, smiling as she demonstrated to me her panic profile. She'd followed her panic attacks to days after she drank intensely and smoked cigarettes-- neither of which had she done over the late spring while at the same time living in her folks' home. Likewise, her caffeine use had risen significantly while at school-- to enable her wake to up for classes in the wake of celebrating around evening time - and her eating regimen had regressed to pizza and doughnuts. She truly would not like to surrender these propensities, however keeping the diary had advised her that her anxiety manifestations are physical, and that quieting her body had defused her panic triggers once previously. Taking consideration again to dispose of CATS (caffeine, liquor, tobacco, sugar + Nutrasweet), Ellie refocused without coming back to prescriptions. The basic principle - deal with the body- - must stay a first need all through treatment for anxiety. Ellie had a noteworthy backslide when she let go of routine self-care.

Specialists who recall that people have bodies just as psyches are a lot likelier to ask routinely about continuous self-care, including rest and exercise. They're additionally all the more ready to enable customers to defeat their hesitance to pursue a self-care schedule. A tip to recollect for female customers who experience a resurgence of side effects regardless of the way that they're dealing with their body is to think about hormonal changes. Pregnancy, baby blues changes, hysterectomy, and interferences in cycles may add to anxiety. The moderate procedure of menopause, which may start over a wide scope of ages, is another factor to consider. Moves in thyroid capacity likewise add to shifts in anxiety. They can happen at any age, and prevail in female customers. Advisors should be especially aware of what may go on in the body when a customer who was formerly doing admirably starts experiencing difficulty.

Technique 2: Breathe.

Ellie and I next looked into her utilization of diaphragmatic breathing to avert the panic. As it turned out, she'd overlooked how supportive breathing had been the point at which we previously began cooperating, and had stopped doing it. Presently, in addition to the fact that she suffered again from panic, however she thought it was too incredible to be in any way calmed simply by breathing profoundly. She'd started to panic simply contemplating inclination panic. I've regularly discovered that when customers state that breathing "doesn't work," this is on the grounds that they haven't figured out how to do it effectively. Or on the other hand once having scholarly it, they've surrendered it when they felt good, accepting that they never again expected to do it. When they feel anxiety returning, they're persuaded that something so straightforward can't in any way, shape or form be extremely successful. Thusly, it's significant for advisors to underscore and reemphasize that breathing will back off or stop the pressure reaction, if the customer will do what needs to be done.

The greatest square to making breathing gen- uinely accommodating is the time it takes to re- hearse it until it turns into an imbued propensi- ty. Most unwinding books instruct customers to work on breathing once per day for 10 minutes, yet I've never discovered a customer who really figured out how to do it from this one, day by day, concentrated portion. I don't instruct customers to relax for extensive periods until they've re- hearsed it for brief periods quite often. I request that they do the cognizant, profound relaxing for around each moment in turn, 10 to 15 times each day, each time they wind up sitting tight for some- thing- - the water to heat up, the telephone to ring, their regular checkup, the line to move at the bank. This will in the long run help them partner breathing with the majority of their environment and exercises. Along these lines, they're bound to really make sure to inhale when anxiety spikes. Ellie required a survey session in breathing to enable her to refocus.

Technique 3: Mindful Awareness.

Since the arrival of her panic attacks, Ellie had likewise started to expect that she'd generally be apprehensive. "All things considered," she stated, "I thought I was restored when I returned to class, and now take a gander at me! I'm always stressed I'll have another panic assault." She'd began to give calamitous understandings to each little, physical sensation- - basically making panic out of vaporous and irrelevant changes in her physical state. A slight chill or a flashing shudder in her stomach was all she expected to begin hyperventilating in dread that panic was en route, which, obviously, expedited it. She expected to stop the cataclysmic reasoning and redirect her consideration away from her body.

Like most on edge individuals when they stress, Ellie was considering the future and wasn't at the time. She felt constrained by her body, which expected her to be watchful for indications of panic. She'd never thought about that she could deal with her body- - and anticipate panic- - by controlling what she did or didn't focus on. In any case, indeed, by changing her center, she could reduce the probability of another panic assault. An awesome method, this basic "careful mindfulness" practice has two basic advances, rehashed a few times.

1. Customers close their eyes and inhale, seeing the body, how the admission of air feels, how the

heart pulsates, and what sensations they have in the gut, and so on.

2. With their eyes still shut, customers deliberately move their mindfulness away from their bodies to all that they can hear or smell or feel through their skin.

By moving mindfulness to and fro a few times between what's happening in their bodies and what's happening around them, customers learn in a physical manner that they can control what parts of their reality - inner or outside - they'll take note. This gives them an inside locus of control, demonstrating them, as Ellie realized, that when they can overlook physical sensations, they can quit making the disastrous elucidations that really expedite panic or stress. It's a basic procedure, which enables them to feel more in charge as they remain aware of the present.

Group Two: Tension, Stress, and Dread

Numerous customers with generalized anxiety disorder (GAD) experience abnormal amounts of strain that are physically awkward and force them to look quickly for the explanations for their anxiety. They trust they can "fathom" whatever issue is by all accounts causing anxiety and accordingly assuage its side effects. Be that as it may, since quite a bit of their increased pressure isn't about a genuine issue, they basically sit around going around their internal labyrinth of self-propagating stress. What's more, regardless of whether their pressure stems from mental or neurobiological causes, there are approaches to wipe out the indications of chronic stress before tending to those measurements. The accompanying techniques are most useful for lessening chronic pressure.

Technique 4: Don't Listen When Worry Calls Your Name.

Colleen dreaded I'd think she was insane when she stated, "Maybe my anxiety has a voice. It calls to me, 'Stress presently,' notwithstanding when there's nothing at the forefront of my thoughts. At that point I need to go searching for what's up." And she was truly adept at discovering something incorrectly to stress over. An official who had a great deal of irons in the flame, she had no lack of undertakings that required her supervision. On quickly, she could stress over whether a report had been right, or anticipated figures were precise, or an agreement would produce pay for her firm. In portraying the voice of stress, she was depicting that physical, pit-of-the-stomach feeling of fate that goes ahead for reasons unknown, and after that propels a clarification for why it's there.

This sentiment of fear and pressure, experienced by most GAD customers, really includes a state of second rate dread, which can likewise cause other physical indications, similar to migraine, temporo-mandibular joint (TMJ) agony, and ulcers.

Maybe a couple understand that the sentiment of fear is only the emotional indication of physical pressure. This "Don't Listen" strategy diminishes this strain by consolidating a choice to disregard the voice of stress with a signal for the unwinding state. From the get-go in treatment, GAD customers learn dynamic muscle unwinding to get alleviation. I generally show them how to sign up unwinding a few times for the duration of the day by drawing a breath and recalling how they feel toward the part of the bargain work out. We for the most part pair that profoundly loosened up state with a shading, picture, and word to fortify relationship with muscle unwinding and make it simpler to prompt the sensation freely.

We at that point utilize that capacity to unwind to check the voice of stress. Customers should initially discover that stress is a propensity with a neurobiological supporting. Notwithstanding when an individual isn't especially stressed over anything, an anxiety-inclined cerebrum can make a feeling of fate, which at that point causes hypervigilance as the individual attempts to make sense of what's up. Colleen grinned with acknowledgment when I said that, when she was in this state, it was as if her cerebrum had gone into radar mode, checking her viewpoints for issues to shield against. I requested that her focus on the request for occasions, and she immediately perceived that the fear happened before she deliberately had a stress. "Be that as it may, she reported, "I generally discover something that could be causing the fate, so I surmise I had a valid justification to stress without acknowledging it."

She accepted the fate/fear must have a genuine reason, and was calmed to discover that her need to discover the reason (when there truly wasn't one) originated from a mind work. This reason looking for part of her mind, triggered by changes in her physiology that made her vibe fear, as a result, got out, "Stress now!"

To quit tuning in to that direction to stress, I recommended that she state to herself, "It's simply my on edge mind terminating incorrectly." This would be the signal for her to start unwinding breathing, which would stop the physical impressions of fear that trigger the radar.

Technique 5: Knowing, Not Showing, Anger.

Outrage can be so anxiety-inciting that a customer may not enable himself to know he's furious. I frequently find that customers with GAD have an undetected dread of being furious. Sway was a valid example. He had such a tight smile, that his grin was about a scowl, and his migraines, tight face muscles, and chronic TMJ issues all recommended he was gnawing back words that could push him into difficulty. There were numerous fields of his life where he felt troubled, for example, missing out on an advancement and his better half's chronic powerlessness to spend inside their financial limit, however he truly accepted he was "putting a decent face" on his issues. Similarly as with different restless customers, the intense anxiety was convincing enough to order the treatment time, and it would have been conceivable to disregard the annoyance association. Be that as it may, insofar as annoyance remains untreated, the on edge customer's indications will remain set up.

At the point when a customer fears outrage due to past involvement - when she recollects the unnerving fierceness of a parent, or was seriously denounced for demonstrating any resentment herself- - the very sentiment of annoyance, despite the fact that it stays oblivious, can deliver anxiety. The way to calming this sort of anxiety is to diminish the customer's feeling of pressure and stress, while raising the cognizance of resentment so it tends to be managed in treatment. I've discovered that basically having the option to feel and confess to outrage in sessions, and to start chipping away at how to securely express it, lessens anxiety. I tell customers, "To know you're furious doesn't expect you to show you're irate."

The strategy is straightforward. I train customers that whenever they're hit with anxiety, they ought to promptly plunk down and compose whatever number answers as would be prudent to this particular inquiry, "In the event that I were irate, what may I be furious about? I instruct them to limit their responses to single words or brief expressions. The speculative idea of the inquiry is a key element, since it doesn't make them feel focused on the possibility that they're furious. They may crush the rundown or get it for dialog, however I ask them to at any rate reveal to me their responses to composing this rundown. As a matter of course, this activity has helped a portion of my on edge customers start to get understanding into the association between their indignation and their anxiety, which opens the entry-way to more profound degrees of psychotherapy that can resolve long-standing resentment issues.

Technique 6: Have a Little Fun.

Chuckling is an incredible method to expand nice sentiments and release pressure. The issue for restless customers is that they pay attention to life with the goal that they quit making fun in their lives, and they quit encountering life's entertaining minutes. Everything turns into a potential issue, as opposed to an approach to feel satisfaction or pleasure.

Margaret was a clever lady, whose amusingness was self-belittling. An abnormal state official who regularly worked 12-to 14-hour days, she'd quit snickering or arranging fun ends of the week around two advancements back. Her better half once in a while observed her on weeknights, and on Saturday and Sunday, she normally disclosed to him she was simply "going to keep running over to the workplace for a brief period"- - somewhere in the range of 3 to 7 hours. When I solicited her to make a rundown from what she accomplished for no particular reason, she was hindered. Other than having a beverage with companions after work, her rundown of charming exercises was practically nonexistent.

Connecting with fun and play isn't simple for the genuine, tense worrier. I've frequently found, in any case, that playing with a kid will get an individual chuckling, so I requested that her invest some energy with her young nieces. She concurred, and saw that she felt progressively loose in the wake of being with them for an evening. At that point I approached her to look for any drive to accomplish something "in light of the fact that," with no specific plan as a top priority. When I saw her next, she appeared to be changed. She stated, "I had a motivation to stop for a frozen treat, so I just went out and got it. I don't have the foggiest idea when the last time was that I wanted to accomplish something and simply did it- - no stresses over whether every other person had a cone or whether I should hold up till later. It was fun!" Over time, tuning in to her internal wishes helped Margaret feel that there was a repository of delight in life that she'd been denying herself, and she started to try different things with giving herself an opportunity to discover it.

In any case, Margaret expected to rediscover what she preferred following quite a while of overlooking delight. For a period, our treatment objective was essentially to relearn what she had a ton of fun doing. Fun-starved customers at times need a "solution," like "Take two hours of satire club and blend with an exceptional companion, when seven days" or "Plan one end of the week away with your better half at regular intervals." as anyone might expect, firmly wired obsessive workers at first need to make fun a genuine objective of treatment, something to be sought after with a portion of a similar stubbornness they put into work.â But once they really end up chuckling and having a good time, they become less firmly wired, not so much hounded, but rather more joyful. Chuckling itself is probably the best medicine of just for strain and anxiety.

Group Three: The Mental Anguish of Rumination

The last techniques are those that manage the troublesome issue of a cerebrum that won't quit considering upsetting contemplations. Stresses prevail in social fear, GAD, and different sorts of anxiety, and ceaseless rumination can make queasiness and strain, obliterating each beneficial thing throughout everyday life. A representation drawn from nature for this sort of stress would be kudzu, the almost plant that multiplies fiercely, choking out each other type of life, similarly as constant stress chokes out customers' psychological and emotional lives.

I don't accept rumination is brought about by profound situated clash in the manner outrage anxiety may be; I believe it's as a rule a neurobiological determined component of anxiety. What customers for the most part stress over - frequently common, everyday concerns- - is less significant than the inescapability of the stress. Their cerebrums keep the stress murmuring along out of sight, producing strain or debilitated sentiments, obliterating fixation, and reducing the ability to focus on the beneficial things throughout every-day life. Looking for consolation or attempting to take care of the issue they're stressing over turns into their sole mental movement, darkening the scene of their lives. Nor can ruminators ever get enough consolation to quit stressing by and large. On the off chance that one stress is settled, another pops straight up- - there's constantly a new "stress of the day."

Treatment with these customers shouldn't con-centrate on a particular stress, yet rather on the demonstration of stressing itself. On the off chance that a ruminating cerebrum resembles a motor stuck in apparatus and overheating, at that point easing back or halting it allows it to chill. The more rumination is interfered with, the more outlandish it'll be to proceed. The accompanying strategies are the best in wiping out rumination.

Technique 7: Turning It Off.

Subsides rumination was the worst thing about his reality. At an impressive rate super salesman with noteworthy drive, he had an ability to fuss that could destroy a less enthusiastic individual. His mind went starting with one conceivable issue then onto the next like a pinball that never stops. Ruminating stress distracted him so much that he couldn't appreciate being with his kids or unwind before resting - his last cognizant mindfulness during the evening was of stress.

In treatment, he experienced considerable difficulties concentrating on only each issue in turn; one stress just helped him to remember one more and again after that. Before tending to the mental underpinnings of stress in his life, we expected to discover a route for Peter to chill off his cerebrum and end the enduring progression of rumination for some time.

I've acquired the idea of "clearing space" to mood killer and calm the ruminative personality. I request that the customer sit discreetly with eyes shut and center around a picture of an open compartment prepared to get each issue at the forefront of their thoughts. She's at that point educated to see and name each issue or stress, and envision placing it into the holder. At the point when no more issues ring a bell, I propose that the customer rationally "put a cover" on the compartment and spot it on a rack or in some other off the beaten path place until she needs to return to get something from it. When the container is on the rack, the customer welcomes into the space left in her mind whatever is the most significant current idea or feeling. Maybe she's at the workplace and necessities to consider a business related issue, or she needs to shop and should arrange for what she'll purchase, or she's with companions and needs to concentrate on what they're stating. Around evening time, directly before rest, the customer is approached to welcome a tranquil idea to concentrate on while floating off.

The objective of "turning it off" is to allow the ruminative personality to rest and quiet down.

Technique 8: Persistent Interruption of Rumination.

Ruminative stress has its very own existence, reliably meddling with each other idea in your customer's psyche. Thought-halting/thought-supplanting is the best subjective treatment procedure for hindering chronic rumination, however

I locate the way to making it work is perseverance. Customers rapidly get on the system itself, yet they're constantly stunned by how rumination can subvert all their great endeavors, and by how tenaciously they need to keep at it to succeed. I've had customers returned and state the method didn't work, since they'd attempted it 20 to multiple times in a day despite everything they were ruminating. I reveal to them that they should do it each time they find themselves ruminating, regardless of whether it is 1,000 times each day or more! That is the thing that I mean by perseverance.

Darla is a genuine model. She was a self-portrayed wet blanket before she got malignancy, yet after her finding, her anxiety zoomed wild. Despite the fact that treatment was fruitful and she'd been going away for quite a while, regardless she had steady, negative, dashing considerations about whether her malignant growth would repeat. An extremely diligent employee in treatment, she did each technique I recommended, and was prepared to utilize thought-halting to interfere with her ruminations about malignancy. "Recollect that," I outlined for her, "triumphant this game is about tirelessness. Do the idea halting activity each and every time you end up stressing, regardless of how often you need to do it."

At the following session, she revealed her prosperity - she truly had profoundly curtailed the measure of stressing she was doing. Be that as it may, it worked simply because I'd cautioned her about how determined she'd must be. "When you disclosed to me I'd need to thought-stop without fail, regardless of whether it was 1,000 times each day," she stated, "I thought you were joking. On the off chance that you hadn't cautioned me, I'd have surrendered in depression after around multiple times, figuring it could never work for me. Since you said 1,000, I figured I would be wise to finish what has been started. Following a few days, it showed signs of improvement." Rumination is constant, and the best way to beat it unexpectedly, as it were, is to be considerably progressively steady.

Technique 9: Worry Well, But Only Once.

A few stresses simply must be confronted head-on, and agonizing over them the correct way can help dispense with optional, pointless stressing. It is realized that next medicinal outcomes were going to recount to the account of whether she required medical procedure. In spite of the fact that there's constantly a degree of genuine stress over any medicinal issue, some ailments, similar to high thyroid, make anxiety symptoms. Connie's therapeutic issues weren't causing the anxiety indications, however her anxiety about her condition was impeding her medicinal recuperation. She called the specialist's office over and over, until the specialist said she'd fire Connie on the off chance that she got one more telephone call before the test outcomes came in.

Connie was crazy with stress, so we evaluated a strategy that really had her stress, yet stress well-- and just once. Here's the manner by which that works. The customer must:

(1) Stress through every one of the issues

(2) Do whatever must be done right now

(3) Set when it'll be important to reconsider the stress

(4) Compose that time on a schedule

(5) At whatever point the idea springs up once more, state, "Stop! I effectively stressed!" and occupy her contemplations as fast as conceivable to another movement.

Connie and I set a 10-minute time limit on our stress session, and afterward together considered all the potential repercussions of a positive test outcome. She secured things, for example, "Who'll watch the feline while I'm in the emergency clinic?""Will I need to miss an excessive number of long periods of work?""Will I need a ride home?" We secured everything from the everyday to the genuine, assuming improbable, "Consider the possibility that I bite the dust while in medical procedure.

It's basic to this technique to consider every contingency, except 10 minutes, shockingly, is a satisfactory measure of time where to do that. Toward the part of the bargain time frame, Connie concurred that she had no different stresses identified with the medical procedure, so we set a period at which she thought she'd have to reconsider the issue. We concurred that whenever she should give the plausibility of medical procedure a chance to enter her thoughts was the point at which the specialist's office called. Until that minute, any idea would be counterproductive. She wrote in her PDA that she could stress again at 4 p.m. on Tuesday evening, by which time the outcomes would be in and the specialist had vowed to call. On the off chance that she hadn't heard by then, at that point she could begin stressing and call the specialist's office.

Having stressed well, we moved to the "Main Once" some portion of the strategy. She at that point rehearsed, "Stop It! I effectively stressed!" and we made a rundown she could bear with her that listed a few diversions to utilize. While this may sound trite, her cerebrum trusted her when she said she'd officially stressed, in light of the fact that it was valid.

Technique 10: Learn to Plan Instead of Worry.

A major contrast among arranging and stressing is that a decent arrangement needn't bother with consistent survey. An on edge mind, in any case, will reexamine an arrangement again and again to be certain it's the correct arrangement. This is all simply ruminating stress camouflaging itself as making an arrangement.

Customers who ruminate about a stress consistently attempt to dispose of it by looking for the consolation that it's unwarranted. They accept that on the off chance that they get the correct sort of answer for their concern - the correct snippet of data or the best consolation - they'll at that point be freed of the stress for the last time. They need to be certain beyond a shadow of a doubt, for instance, that a minor slip-up they made at work won't bring about their being terminated. As a general rule, be that as it may, a ruminating cerebrum will essentially discover some blemish in the most safeguard consolation and set the customer off on the track of looking for a shockingly better one.

One great approach to escape the consolation trap is to utilize the basics of arranging. This straightforward yet regularly ignored aptitude can have a major effect in quieting a ruminative personality. I show individuals how to supplant stressing with arranging. For most, this incorporates:

(1) Solidly recognizing an issue

(2) Posting the critical thinking alternatives

(3) Picking one of the choices

(4) Working out a game plan.

To be fruitful with this methodology, customers should likewise have figured out how to apply the idea halting/thought-supplanting instruments, or they'll transform arranging into unlimited cycles of re-planning.

After they make an arrangement, ruminating customers will feel better for a couple of minutes and afterward start "exploring the arrangement"- - a standard mental stunt of their anxiety disorder.

The rumination makes them feel overpowered, which triggers their craving for consolation. In any case, when they've really made the arrangement, they can utilize the way that they have the arrangement as a solid consolation to forestall the round-robin of ruminative re-planning. The arrangement turns out to be a piece of the idea halting statement, "Stop! I have an arrangement!" It additionally helps stop unending consolation chasing, in light of the fact that it gives composed arrangements even to issues the ruminator thought about miserably perplexing.

For instance, if Connie, who'd stressed well over medical procedure, discovered she had to have the medical procedure, she could work out the arrangement to prepare. The new arrangement would cover every one of the issues she'd recognized in her stress session, from finding a cat-sitter to composing a living will. She'd put culmination dates in for each progression and check off the things as she did them until the day of the medical procedure. At that point, each time she required consolation, the solid proof that she had a decent arrangement would empower her to go on to some other idea or action.

While these procedures aren't entangled or actually hard to instruct, they do require persistence and assurance from both specialist and customer. For best outcomes, they likewise request clinical learning of how and why they work, and with what sorts of issues; they can't just be utilized as generally useful applications, useful for anyone in any situation.

Be that as it may, the prizes of showing individuals how to utilize these misleadingly basic, undramatic, and ungimmicky strategies are incredible. While customers in this culture have been taught to need and anticipate immediate help from their distress at the fly of a pill, we can demonstrate them we have something better to offer. We can give individuals their very own enduring feeling force and skill by helping them figure out how to function effectively with their very own indications, to vanquish anxiety through their own endeavors - and do this in a non-manipulative, conscious, connecting way. Individuals like discovering that they have some authority over their sentiments; it gives them increasingly self-assurance to know they're not the captives of physiological excitement or runaway mental examples. What's more, what we instruct them resembles playing the piano or riding a bike: they possess it forever; it turns into a piece of their human collection. What medicine can make that guarantee?

Chapter Six

Declutter your mind

Around Weekly ago I got up one morning to perform some work at your home on the laptop. I had my whole day planned out. However, I did not comply with this program. As an alternative I spent approximately 6 hours hammering out my residence.

I did not Only devote the hours hoovering, washing or polishing. I spent all those hours draining out all of the accumulated bits and bobs which each and every house hastens.

I stuffed with a few bags for charity, so I moved into the Recycling lender. I came across fresh discreet domiciles for items infrequently found, and cleared drawers out of things that I hadn't ever seen before!

I re arranged and tidied computersand found new homes for publication shelves and table mats!

The Awareness of relief after I'd completed that is good. Your home felt lighter, airier, I'd almost doubled the distance inside my property. I'd re-moved out crap and that I felt for this.

I'd spring cleaned.

Although not only had I spring cleaned my own residence, I'd spring washed myself.

I figure that emphasized me I had a spring wash was that which happened in the post office the afternoon before.

I Had visited place my sister's birthday cardand it was just when I had been on the road home I realized I'd left a bag behind me at the post office. I hadn't ever done this before, I had been always aware and alert of everything I had been carrying out and that I hadn't ever left anything behind. It had been okay, " I got back the bag a day later, however it made me considering simply how diverted I'd been. You maybe wondering what's this related to clearing out a residence.

Look back within the initial publication you Received - Life Review. I asked was there that a space you had to declutter. Whenever you head in to a room that's cluttered and cluttered or cluttered, this could have an immediate effect in your own emotions, also in your own degree of energy.

Think about a hotel room once you first walkin. It Really Is Tidy, tidy, you really feel immediately relaxed. You sleep soundly init and get dressed and shop around today, its cluttered, and also you also don't get that feeling of comfort as you did earlier. (But the chambermaid is available from and fixes it)

However, I'm maybe not mainly speaking about cleanup. I'm discussing Clearing. Your physical environment possess a direct and indirect influence on your mood. In reality at the very first life training session we all discover of a individual's physical atmosphere, to estimate how it's impacting their joy, and also their awareness of energy.

I really do a Whole Lot of non client Work at home. Yet my house has been littered with things I didn't want anymore. It'd areas which were cluttered and maybe not employed in the ideal approach. The areas believed dull and packed and maybe not conducive to some stream of thoughts!

Can your property promote calm and restfulness? Can be the living area bright, cheerful, and bright?

Can you feel rested when you walk in to a space? Or does one push the clutter a side, push items into full cupboards? Are the clothes and personal ramifications in disarray? Would you discover what you're interested in when you desire this, or must you hunt and hunt?

You visit Life training is just as much centered on the technical aspect of life because it's the mental side. They affect one other. Directly and non-directly.

If You're struggling with work, customs, Finance, all it really is, and you're working or living at a messy, dirty or cluttered ecosystem, it will not lift up you to an area of calm and peacefulness at which you're able to change view and view your choices.

Think about a song you despise. Imagine Hearing this tune Repeatedly and over. It will force you demented. You certainly wouldn't feel relaxed and calm. Now imagine hearing your own preferred relaxing songs. You'd feel relaxed since you're engaging your sensory sensations and also the relaxing music gets the consequence of relaxing you personally.

And therefore it really is for your own Visual senses. Look up on a Cluttered dirty room and also you may feel stressed, annoyed or downright pissed off. Look up on a room that's tidy and neat and also you feel that the distance and also the willingness. The space does not need to be decorated. Just clean and fresh and clean is going to do just fine. Be kind to your visual sensations along with your body and emotions will probably benefit.

Ask Your self, do you rather sit at an area and gaze up on jumble and disarray, or sit at an area and gaze up on tidiness and brightness? To provide yourself mind space, you want to check out your living area, and find out whether it's detrimental to your emotional wellbeing, or even beneficial.

The Only way you need to understand I speak the facts are to just take 1 room at one time on the upcoming month and clean it out of items that you never desire or desire. Physically clean your distance, and determine how your time improves when you're within the space, and also the way your mood is milder and much more stimulating.

Bedroom - be certain that the corners on your room are away from any items, this opens the feeling of distance. Colourco ordinate your laundry on your wardrobe so when you start the wardrobe from the morning you're greeted with an organized variety of one's clothes as opposed to the usual mishmash of items which you may scarcely discern.

Bathroom as far as you can, Have the counters clean, also in the event that you're able to purchase just a tiny unit, then put all of your valuables inside that. Place a candle or 2 and sometimes possibly a vase of dried flowers inside the restroom.

Kitchen get rid of older invoices and Letters, drive out all of the cupboards of those single pieces and bobs, every thing that mount up to nothing!!

Living space - exactly what does not Have to maintain there, you're able to remove and look for a much suitable dwelling for. Tidy your dvds and videos. You'll understand your self exactly what you need or desire in there and what's merely consuming space.

Your entire aim is to De clutter. By de-cluttering your physical ecosystem, you're ordering your mood and emotions. You're allowing your distance to become more relaxing and inviting. You're indicating your brain that you simply deserve beauty and niceties.

Life is about doing the Tiny things which include Quality and improvement to your own life and in addition taking advantage of what you've got.

When experts discuss diet, they counsel to start small, make modest alterations.

And thus it's exactly the exact same here. Making Small very little changes which increase the level of one's living space, adds Up to modifications on a larger scale on your mood and emotions. Check It out and Watch for your self!

Emotional focus is the most essential skill in regards to success in virtually any area of one's own life. For the time being, let us consider exactly the mental attention is critical for success and just how it is able to aid you do it.

Focus keeps distractions from increasing

We all get sidetracked by new tasks, matters that want care of across the workplace or at the house, and ofcourse by family associates and colleagues. There is always something else which will require our attention, or even a fun new task we'd actually quite be taking care of.

This really is where attention can make a substantial differentiation and allow you to do it. Focus looks like a pair of blinders. It will help you concentrate on the job available until it's done.

Focus told you from getting mistakes

You are less likely to create errors because of the simple fact you are not continuously side-tracked and also you're providing your entire focus to anything it's you're taking care of at the moment. If your attention is broken and you are not totally engaged and immersed at the job you're working onerrors occur.

Being concentrated, alternatively, assists you pay attention to work. It allows one to create less errors to begin with once you do create sure they are if you are not side-tracked, you are that a lot more likely to catch them and repair them.

Focus is certainly a critical to an effective frame of mind. Continuously educate your self of precisely what your organization has to complete together, what its role is, and you're doing this. Continue focusing on your own objectives using them somewhere which you're able to observe them.

Conclusion result is a much greater quality thing, regardless of what you are handling.

Focus will help you get more done faster

If you are exceptionally focused (thanks to this looming as date)a job which could normally require one half an evening is suddenly achieved in half an hour. On top of that, the final outcome is often far better than you are normal work as you are exceptionally focused and therefore are becoming in to the flow where anything comes together virtually readily.

Forged to brain-wave sound that assists you concentrate

Sound with particular brain-wave sounds will set you in a country of ultra attention and have better in less time naturally. Brainwave entrainment music can even be played throughout tasks as work and sometimes sports.

Stress and anxiety are basic encounters for a great many people. Truth be told, 70% of grown-ups in the US state they feel pressure or anxiety day by day.

Here are some basic approaches to calm pressure and anxiety.

1. Exercise

Exercise is one of the most significant things you can do to battle pressure. It may appear to be conflicting, yet putting physical weight on your body through exercise can diminish mental pressure. The advantages are most grounded when you practice normally. Individuals who exercise routinely are more averse to encounter anxiety than the individuals who don't exercise\

There are a couple of purposes for this:

•Stress hormones: Exercise brings down your body's pressure hormones —, for example, cortisol — over the long haul. It additionally helps discharge endorphins, which are synthetic substances that improve your disposition and go about as characteristic painkillers.

•Sleep: Exercise can likewise improve your rest quality, which can be adversely influenced by pressure and anxiety.

•Confidence: When you practice consistently, you may feel increasingly able and certain about your body, which thusly advances mental prosperity.

Attempt to discover an activity routine or movement you appreciate, for example, strolling, moving, shake climbing or yoga.

Exercises —, for example, strolling or running — that include redundant developments of huge muscle gatherings can be especially pressure assuaging.

2. Think about Supplements

A few enhancements advance pressure and anxiety decrease. Here is a short review of probably the most widely recognized ones:

•Lemon analgesic: Lemon salve is an individual from the mint family that has been read for its enemy of anxiety impacts

•Omega-3 unsaturated fats: One examination demonstrated that restorative understudies who got omega-3 enhancements encountered a 20% decrease in anxiety manifestations

•Ashwagandha: Ashwagandha is a herb utilized in Ayurvedic drug to treat pressure and anxiety. A few examinations propose that it's powerful

•Green tea: Green tea contains numerous polyphenol cancer prevention agents which give medical advantages. It might lower pressure and anxiety by expanding serotonin levels

•Valerian: Valerian root is a prevalent tranquilizer because of its sedating impact. It contains valerenic corrosive, which adjusts gamma-aminobutyric corrosive (GABA) receptors to bring down anxiety.

•Kava: kava is a psychoactive individual from the pepper family. Since a long time ago utilized as a narcotic in the South Pacific, it is progressively utilized in Europe and the US to treat mellow pressure and anxiety

A few enhancements can communicate with drugs or have reactions, so you might need to counsel with a specialist on the off chance that you have an ailment.

Shop for ashwagandha, omega-3 enhancements, green tea, and lemon emollient on the web.

3. Light a Candle

Utilizing fundamental oils or consuming a scented light may help diminish your sentiments of stress and anxiety.

A few aromas are particularly calming. Here are the absolute most quieting fragrances:

- Lavender

- Rose

- Vetiver

- Bergamot

- Roman chamomile

- Neroli

- Frankincense

- Sandalwood

- Ylangylang

- Orange or orange bloom

- Geranium

Utilizing aromas to treat your temperament is called fragrance based treatment. A few investigations demonstrate that fragrance based treatment can diminish anxiety and improve rest

4. Diminish Your Caffeine Intake

Caffeine is a stimulant found in espresso, tea, chocolate and caffeinated drinks. High dosages can build anxiety Individuals have various limits for how much caffeine they can endure. In the event that you see that caffeine makes you jumpy or on edge, consider curtailing. Albeit numerous examinations demonstrate that espresso can be solid with some restraint, it's not for everybody. As a rule, five or less cups for each day is viewed as a moderate sum.

5. Record It

One approach to deal with pressure is to record things. While recording what you're worried about is one methodology, another is writing down what you're thankful for. Appreciation may help mitigate pressure and anxiety by concentrating your musings on what's sure in your life.

6. Bite Gum

For an excessively simple and brisk pressure reliever, have a go at biting a stick of gum. One investigation demonstrated that individuals who bit gum had a more noteworthy feeling of prosperity and lower pressure. One conceivable clarification is that biting gum causes cerebrum waves like those of loosened up individuals. Another is that biting gum elevates blood stream to your cerebrum. Also, one ongoing investigation found that pressure help was most prominent when individuals bitten all the more firmly.

7. Invest Energy With Friends and Family

Social help from loved ones can enable you to overcome unpleasant occasions. Being a piece of a companion system gives you a feeling of having a place and self-esteem, which can help you in intense occasions. One examination found that for ladies specifically, investing energy with companions and youngsters helps discharge oxytocin, a characteristic pressure reliever. This impact is classified "tend and become a close acquaintance with," and is something contrary to the battle or-flight reaction. Remember that the two people profit by fellowship.

Another investigation found that people with the least social associations were bound to experience the ill effects of sorrow and anxiety

8. Chuckle

It's difficult to feel on edge when you're giggling.

It's useful for your wellbeing, and there are a couple of ways it might help ease pressure:

•Relieving your pressure reaction.

•Relieving strain by loosening up your muscles.

In the long haul, chuckling can likewise help improve your insusceptible framework and state of mind. An investigation among individuals with malignant growth found that individuals in the chuckling intercession gathering experienced more pressure help than the individuals who were basically occupied take a stab at viewing an interesting TV show or spending time with companions who make you giggle.

9. Figure out how to Say No

Not all stressors are inside your control, however some are. Assume responsibility for an amazing pieces that you can change and are causing you stress. One approach to do this might be to state "no" more regularly. This is particularly valid on the off chance that you end up taking on beyond what you can deal with, as shuffling numerous obligations can leave you feeling overpowered. Being specific about what you take on — and disapproving of things that will pointlessly add to your heap — can lessen your feelings of anxiety.

10. Figure out how to Avoid Procrastination

Another approach to assume responsibility for your pressure is to remain over your needs and quit dawdling. Dawdling can lead you to act re-sponsively, leaving you scrambling to get up to speed. This can cause pressure, which adversely influences your wellbeing and rest quality (16). Start making a plan for the day composed by need. Give yourself sensible due dates and work your way down the rundown. Work on the things that need to complete today and give yourself lumps of continuous time, as exchanging between undertakings or performing multiple tasks can be upsetting itself.

11. Take a Yoga Class

Yoga has turned into a prevalent strategy for stress help and exercise among all age gatherings. While yoga styles contrast, most offer a shared objective — to join your body and psyche. Yoga principally does this by expanding body and breath mindfulness.

A few investigations have analyzed yoga's impact on emotional well-being. Generally, investigate has discovered that yoga can improve state of mind and may even be as successful as energizer drugs at treating misery and anxiety. Be that as it may, a significant number of these investigations are restricted, and there are still inquiries concerning how yoga attempts to achiev

12. Practice Mindfulness

Care portrays rehearses that stay you to the present minute. It can help battle the anxiety-prompting impacts of negative reasoning. There are a few strategies for expanding care, including care based psychological treatment, care based pressure decrease, yoga and contemplation. An ongoing report in undergrads recommended that care may help increment confidence, which thus decreases manifestations of anxiety and sadness

When all is said in done, the advantage of yoga for stress and anxiety is by all accounts identified with its impact on your sensory system and stress reaction. It might help lower cortisol levels, circulatory strain and pulse and increment gamma-aminobutyric corrosive (GABA), a synapse that is brought down in mind-set disorders.

13. Snuggle

Snuggling, kissing, embracing and sex would all be able to help assuage pressure

Positive physical contact can help discharge oxytocin and lower cortisol. This can help lower circulatory strain and pulse, the two of which are physical indications of stress. Curiously, people aren't the main creatures who snuggle for pressure help. Chimpanzees likewise snuggle companions who are focused

14. Tune in to Soothing Music

Tuning in to music can have an exceptionally loosening up impact on the body. Slow-paced instrumental music can incite the unwinding reaction by helping lower pulse and pulse just as pressure hormones. A few types of traditional, Celtic, Native American and Indian music can be especially relieving, however essentially tuning in to the music you appreciate is successful as well. Nature sounds can likewise be very quieting. This is the reason they're frequently joined into unwinding and reflection music.

15. Profound Breathing

Mental pressure enacts your thoughtful sensory system, flagging your body to go into "battle or-flight" mode. During this response, stress hormones are discharged and you experience physical side effects, for example, a quicker heartbeat, faster breathing and tightened veins. Profound breathing activities can help enact your parasympathetic sensory system, which controls the unwinding reaction.

There are a few types of profound breathing activities, including diaphragmatic breathing, stomach breathing, and gut breathing and paced breath.

The objective of profound breathing is to concentrate your mindfulness on your breath, making it increasingly slow. When you take in profoundly through your nose, your lungs completely grow and your tummy rises. This eases back your pulse, enabling you to feel increasingly quiet.

16. Invest Energy with Your Pet

Having a pet may help diminish pressure and improve your mind-set. Associating with pets may help discharge oxytocin, a cerebrum synthetic that advances a positive state of mind, having a pet may likewise help ease worry by giving you reason, keeping you dynamic and giving friendship — all characteristics that help lessen anxiety.

Recouping emotionally from debacle

Debacles, for example, storms, tremors, transportation mishaps or out of control fires are regularly startling, abrupt and overpowering. For some individuals, there are no ostensibly unmistakable indications of physical damage, yet there can be regardless an emotional toll. It is normal for individuals who have encountered calamity to have compelling emotional responses. Understanding reactions to upsetting occasions can enable you to adapt viably to your emotions, musings and practices, and help you along the way to recuperation.

What are basic responses and reactions to consider

Following debacle, individuals much of the time feel dazed, muddled or incapable to coordinate troubling data. When these underlying responses die down, individuals can encounter an assortment of contemplations and practices. Regular reactions can be:

•Intense or flighty emotions. You might be restless, apprehensive, overpowered or despondency stricken. You may likewise feel more peevish or testy than expected.

•Changes to considerations and standards of conduct. You may have rehashed and striking recollections of the occasion. These recollections may happen for no obvious explanation and may prompt physical responses, for example, fast heartbeat or perspiring. It might be hard to focus or decide. Rest and eating designs likewise can be disturbed — a few people may gorge and sleep in, while others experience lost rest and loss of hunger.

•Sensitivity to ecological elements. Alarms, boisterous commotions, consuming scents or other ecological sensations may invigorate recollections of the fiasco making uplifted anxiety. These "triggers" might be joined by fears that the upsetting occasion will be rehashed.

•Strained relational connections. Expanded clash, for example, progressively visit conflicts with relatives and collaborators, can happen. You may likewise wind up pulled back, disconnected or separated from your standard social exercises.

•Stress-related physical manifestations. Migraines, queasiness and chest agony may happen and could require therapeutic consideration. Prior ailments could be influenced by fiasco related pressure.

How would I adapt?

Luckily, look into demonstrates that the vast majority are strong and after some time can bob over from disaster. It is normal for individuals to experience worry in the quick outcome, yet inside a couple of months the vast majority can resume working as they did preceding the catastrophe. Remember that strength and recuperation are the standard, not delayed pain.

There are various advances you can take to construct emotional prosperity and increase a feeling of control following a calamity, including the accompanying:

•Give yourself an opportunity to modify. Envision that this will be a troublesome time in your life. Enable yourself to grieve the misfortunes you have encountered and attempt to be quiet with changes in your emotional state.

•Ask for help from individuals who care about you and who will tune in and sympathize with your situation. Social backing is a key segment to catastrophe recuperation. Family and companions can be a significant asset. You can discover backing and shared opinion from those who've likewise endure the catastrophe. You may likewise need to contact others not included who might have the option to give more noteworthy help and objectivity.

•Communicate your experience. Express what you are feeling in the ways feel good to you —, for example, conversing with family or dear companions, keeping a journal or taking part in an inventive movement (e.g., drawing, forming dirt, and so on.).

•Find a nearby care group driven by suitably prepared and experienced experts. Care groups are as often as possible accessible for survivors. Gathering exchange can enable you to under-stand that you are not the only one in your re-sponses and feelings. Care group gatherings can be particularly useful for individuals with restrict-ed individual emotionally supportive networks.

•Engage in solid practices to improve your capac-ity to adapt to inordinate pressure. Eat well-ad-justed suppers and get a lot of rest. On the off chance that you experience continuous troubles with rest, you might have the option to discover some alleviation through unwinding strategies. Keep away from liquor and medications since they can be a desensitizing redirection that could reduce just as defer dynamic adapting and push-ing ahead from the debacle.

•Establish or restore schedules. This can incor-porate eating dinners at normal occasions, resting and waking on a standard cycle, or following an activity program. Work in some positive schedules to have something to anticipate during these troubling occasions, such as seeking after a pastime, strolling through an appealing park or neighborhood, or perusing a decent book.

•Avoid settling on real life choices. Exchanging professions or occupations and other significant choices will in general be exceptionally unpleasant in their own privilege and much harder to take on when you're recuperating from a fiasco.

Taking Good Care Of Yourself

Since you've settled on the choice to start your adventure to recuperation, underneath are a few apparatuses to help you all the while. Distinguishing devices and creating plans will enable you to be increasingly arranged and engaged to make a move with regards to your recuperation. Here are sound strides to take:

Moving in the direction of Goals

Individuals in recuperation offer the accompanying proposals:

•Focus on your qualities.

•Focus on taking care of issues.

•Focus on the future as opposed to surveying harms from an earlier time.

•Focus on your life rather than your ailment.

As you take a shot at your recuperation, you should record a portion of your primary objectives. These objectives can be present moment and effectively attainable, or you can begin distinguishing greater, all the more long haul objectives that you need to work your way towards.

It's useful to consider little strides to take toward them over a specific measure of time, similar to a week or a month. Make sure to salute yourself for any triumphs. Accomplishing objectives - even little ones - is an indication of expectation and achievement.

Creating objectives for recuperation can be dubious, particularly on the off chance that you aren't sure what it is that you need to achieve. Think about your interests, things that bring you happiness and things that keep you spurred. Likewise, consider the things you need, similar to where you need your life to go or what you would accomplish a greater amount of in the event that you could. Having a profound interest in the objectives that you set will expand the odds of finishing them.

When you have define objectives for yourself, you have to make sense of what things are important to achieve those objectives. Be clear regarding why you define this objective and how your life will be diverse once this objective is accomplished. You ought to likewise consider the qualities and abilities that you have that will enable you to accomplish your objective. Attempt to include important emotionally supportive networks and assets that can help you through the procedure if and when you need it. At long last, make sure to remain concentrated on the objective and not on the troubles you may have. Keep a receptive outlook, and realize that you may hit boundaries en route. Recuperation is no simple errand, and concentrating on the negative encounters will just make things harder.

Make a diary or scrapbook with pictures and clippings to help keep up your objectives. Keeping a diary or scrapbook is a decent method to follow your objectives and help you to remember the things you've achieved and the things despite everything you intend to achieve. Keep on including new astoundingly up. Recuperation is a consistent procedure and proceeding to set objectives for yourself will keep you spurred to reach and look after wellbeing.

Care For Yourself

Taking great consideration of yourself is fundamental to the achievement of your recuperation procedure. Individuals in recuperation find that their physical, profound, and emotional wellbeing are altogether associated, and that supporting one bolsters the others. Dealing with all parts of you will improve the probability that you remain well.

To help bolster you in your recuperation, you can get to a three-minute screening device and progress screen for discouragement, anxiety, bipolar disorder, and PTSD. Snap here to take the screener or imprint your advancement.

A few hints for self-care include:

•Live Healthy, eat well nourishments, get enough rest, practice consistently, and keep away from medications and liquor. Oversee pressure and go for standard medicinal registration.

•Practice great cleanliness. Great cleanliness is significant for social, restorative, and mental reasons in that it diminishes the danger of ailment, yet it additionally improves the manner in which others see you and how you see yourself.

•See companions to construct your feeling of having a place. Consider joining a care group to make new companions.

•Try to accomplish something you appreciate each day. That may mean moving, viewing a most loved TV appear, working in the nursery, painting or perusing.

•Find approaches to unwind, similar to contemplation, yoga, getting a back rub, scrubbing down or strolling in the woods.

Reinforce Your Connections

The significance of consolidating bliss, soul, and unwinding in your life has numerous ramifications in creating flexibility (the capacity to recoup from a disease) and remaining solid. The four C's to bliss, soul, and unwinding are: interface with yourself, associate with others, associate with your locale, and make euphoria and fulfillment. As you utilize these four C's make sure to keep attempting to push your solace levels and do things you might not have done before.

Having a banter With Yourself

It is significant that you check in with yourself intermittently. In the event that you don't, at that point you may not understand that things are changing or gaining out of power. Checking in with yourself permits you the chance to assess where you are in your recuperation. You may find that you have to straighten out what venture of your activity plan you are on or attempt distinctive adapting devices.

In the event that you have had low occasions in the past you see how hard it tends to be to escape those spots. Realizing all that you can about your emotional well-being condition will help told you that your tough occasions are not your issue. Making a rundown of achievements that you have accomplished is a decent asset to go back to when you are feeling low.

Another device that may help you is to diary about your encounters. Keeping a diary is an incredible method to find out about yourself. Being totally genuine in your diary is significant; in your diary, you should don't hesitate to allow you to protect down. This will enable you to find how you truly feel and vent your worry in a non-compromising way.

Another technique for interfacing with yourself is to turn into a promoter and offer your story. There has been a great deal of research that investigates the intensity of narrating as a type of treatment. Sharing your very own encounters through composition or talking is a significant phase of recuperation. Similarly as you are bolstered by perusing the musings and encounters of others you can likewise be the individual that helps lift another.

Interface With Others

Investing energy with constructive, cherishing individuals you care about and trust can simplicity stress, help your state of mind and improve the manner in which you feel by and large. They might be relatives, dear companions, individuals from a care group or a friend instructor at the nearby drop-in focus. Numerous people group even have warmlines (free hotlines kept running by individuals with psychological wellness conditions) that you can call to converse with somebody and get companion support.

Research focuses to the advantages of social association:

•Increased satisfaction. In one convincing examination, a key distinction between exceptionally cheerful individuals and less upbeat individuals was great connections.

•Better wellbeing. Dejection was related with a higher danger of hypertension in an ongoing investigation of more seasoned individuals.

•A longer life. Individuals with solid social and network ties were a few times less inclined to kick the bucket during a 9-year study

Association happens when you get:

•Concrete help, for example, having a companion lift your children up from school;

•Emotional support, such as hearing somebody state, "I'm extremely sorry you're having such an intense time";

•Perspective, such as being reminded that even the moodiest young people grow up;

•Advice, for example, a recommendation to design a week by week date with your mate;

•Validation, such as discovering that different people love perusing train plans as well.

Do you have enough help? Inquire as to whether you have at any rate a couple of companions or relatives who:

•You feel good to be with;

•Give you a feeling that you could disclose to them anything;

•Can help you take care of issues;

•Make you feel esteemed;

•Take your worries genuinely.

Close Banter With Your Community

An incredible method to feel emotionally solid and flexible in the midst of stress is to feel associated with an expansive network. Consider the things you like to do. You can grow your informal organization by investigating a network association that unites individuals who offer similar premiums. For example, numerous networks have neighborhood biking, climbing, or strolling gatherings. Is there something you've for the longest time been itching to do like gain proficiency with another dialect? Take a class, or join a nearby gathering. You likewise may discover the help you need through nearby care groups for a particular issue like child rearing, managing a medical issue, or thinking about a friend or family member who's evil.

Or on the other hand consider volunteering with a network association that helps fill a need. Here are a few hints to ensure your volunteer experience works for you, and doesn't turn into an extra wellspring of stress:

•Get the correct match. Consider what sort of work you like to do, in light of your interests, aptitudes and accessibility. Think about making this a rundown for simpler intelligibility. Do you like to peruse, compose, manufacture things, fix things, or sort and arrange? Do you have an extraordinary field of learning that you could educate to battling understudies as a guide or mentor? Is it true that you are particularly worried about vagrancy or contamination? Do you want to garden or work in an office? Do you communicate in another dialect? Do you should be at home, and carry your humanitarian effort home with you? Whatever your circumstance and your interests, there is most likely a volunteer chance to make an extraordinary commitment in your locale. Volunteering will enable you to manufacture solid associations with others - a demonstrated method to ensure your psychological wellness.

•Make it tally. You need your volunteer time to have any kind of effect, so pose inquiries to ensure the association uses volunteers effectively and gainfully. Ask what volunteers do, where and when they do it, and whether a worker is accessible with data and direction when required.

•Find an association. To locate a volunteer position that is directly for you, contact your volunteer focus. Look in the Yellow Pages under "Volunteer Clearinghouse" or "Volunteer Center," at your nearby wellbeing office additionally might search for volunteers. You can likewise contact your city or province data line to request a referral to a volunteer organizer administration in your general vicinity.

Chapter Seven

CONCLUSION

A panic assault can happen for apparently no explanation and has been portrayed by sufferers as the most alarming background of their life. On the off chance that you have ever encountered this you likely need to know one thing rapidly, would you be able to fix panic attacks? A great many people will involvement with least one panic assault in their lifetime, anyway for other people, panic attacks become a piece of their regular daily existence. This every day panic leaves them edgy to fix panic attacks so they can continue an ordinary life.

Restoring these attacks is definitely not a straight-forward thing; it isn't simply a question of taking an enemy of panic pill and proceeding onward. You should survey your specific manifestations and causes with a restorative expert and after that settle on an appropriate activity plan. These attacks have been known to be misdiagnosed since other ailments can firmly imitate them. Respiratory failures, stroke and hyperthyroidism would all be able to have comparative indications and ought to be precluded before you endeavor to fix anxiety attacks throughout your life.

There is a particular arrangement of criteria used to analyze these attacks in people and an appropriate appraisal must be finished. The criteria incorporates however isn't restricted to; rehashed attacks, at any rate one assault pursued by a month of steady worry over having another assault, stress over going insane or changing your conduct as a result of the attacks. Notwithstanding the above criteria, the attacks must not be related with another disorder, for example, over the top habitual disorder (OCD) or incited by medication misuse.

You are having a panic assault, you feel as though you are going to black out, and your head is turning near and the air is getting thick. You are feeling alarmed, this is the subsequent panic assault in one day. Relieving panic attacks needs to turn into your main need. You are not the only one, a huge number of people experience the ill effects of anxiety and panic disorders. A panic assault can happen whenever, and there is normally a trigger that makes it happen. Panic attacks don't separate, they can happen anyplace and to anybody. There are two strategies that can be utilized to fix panic attacks.

CPSIA information can be obtained
at www.ICGtesting.com
Printed in the USA
LVHW080506310822
727186LV00008B/391